CROCHET Lace

CROCHET *Lace*

Techniques, Patterns, and Projects

Pauline Turner

Dover Publications, Inc.
Mineola, New York

I would like to express my grateful thanks to Anita, Asa, Dorothy, Maureen, Rita, and Tracey. They were invaluable in encouraging and supporting me in this project.

Photographs: Syd Cumbus
Diagrams: Keith Aubrey
Additional crochet: Anita Shepherd, Dorothy Burton, Rita Williams

Bibliographical Note

Crochet Lace: Techniques, Patterns, and Projects, first published by Dover Publications, Inc., in 2015, is an unabridged republication of *Crocheted Lace,* originally published in 2003 by Martingale & Company, Woodinville, Washington.

Library of Congress Cataloging-in-Publication Data

Turner, Pauline.
     Crochet lace : techniques, patterns, and projects / Pauline Turner.
          pages cm
     Originally published: Martingale, 2003.
     ISBN-13: 978-0-486-79457-0
     ISBN-10: 0-486-79457-1
     1. Lace and lace making—Patterns. 2. Crocheting—Patterns. I. Title.
     TT800.T87 2015
     746.43'4—dc23
                                                                    2014036270

Manufactured in the United States by Courier Corporation
79457101   2015
www.doverpublications.com

Contents

Introduction

With any craft there will always be confusion about its exact source or starting point, often because an idea beginning in one country will quickly be available in another. As I searched for when crochet arrived in Britain, and as I tried to find the journey it made to get to Britain, I realized that there was a conflict of opinions. By searching further, it became clear that assumptions had been made that only served to confuse matters and that even basic definitions varied.

I began looking in dictionaries and encyclopedias to see how they described crochet. There was very little to choose between them. The entry in the *Chambers Twentieth Century Dictionary*, which I felt gave as concise a definition as any, states that crochet is looping work done with a small hook. Nowadays, the word *small* is unnecessary because crochet can employ huge hooks on which to work rug wool and very thick string. However, this book focuses on thread crochet and therefore the word *small* is appropriate.

Originally, crochet used fine cottons in an attempt to copy the designs of traditional lace. Small hooks with tiny barbed heads were required to manipulate the threads. After the First World War, crocheters started to use thicker threads for crochet work and also fine knitting yarns for greater speed. When rayon was introduced, which split when knitted, it was found that a slightly larger crochet hook worked well with it.

During the late 1960s and early 1970s, new crochet techniques were explored, as was the use of materials other than traditional cotton and linen threads. It was then that the range of hook sizes greatly expanded. Since the 1980s, the variety of hooks has extended further, with increasingly larger sizes, being produced to allow for thicker wool such as rug wool, and baler twine, acrylics, and rag strips to make a variety of useful and decorative articles. Ribbons, wire, and even toilet paper can be used for crochet. However, there is still a lot of speculation over where and when crochet was developed. Part of this confusion occurs because crochet is frequently linked with knitting, and therefore erroneous assumptions are made that crochet is as old as knitting. If this were true and if, as seems likely, the craft of crochet started on the continent of Europe, it seems very strange that there are no paintings or writings describing crochet—particularly since there are paintings of people knitting. Large numbers of beautiful Renaissance paintings show ladies making lace with bobbins on a pillow or with the needle, but none show them crocheting. A rare reference can be found in *Mary Thomas's Knitting Book* when she describes the way the shepherds of Landes in southern France produced knitting using hooked needles made from umbrella ribs. However, the South American natives also used hooked needles with which to knit, not crochet.

The Great Exhibition of 1851, held in London, was famous for exhibiting crafts of all kinds. What is fascinating is the large number of entries in all needlecraft sections except crochet. In fact, the crochet section was included under embroidery. This is another factor indicating that crochet is the youngest of all the needlecraft textiles, and it confirms my understanding that crochet originated from the craft of tambour embroidery, the tambour hook evolving into the crochet hook. The majority of the exhibits came from central and southern England, with single exhibits from Ireland and Liverpool and two from Yorkshire. Each time I find a date for a piece of crochet, it confirms that the craft spread from the continent north, east, and west. It also indicates to me that crochet was not as widespread as it is sometimes said to be.

As I went through the Great Exhibition catalog, I was intrigued to notice that Cornelia Mee had exhibited many pieces of needlework but did not include any crochet. Considering Cornelia Mee was a prolific producer of crochet patterns during the last two decades of the nineteenth century, I find it fascinating that she had not discovered the crochet (or tambour) hook at this point in her creative career.

The following were entries from the catalog of the Great Exhibition of 1851:

Riego de la Branchardaise; Eleonore, London; Inventor and manufacturer exhibiting lace berth, altar cloth, prayer book covers, collars.

Clarke, Eliza; Norwich; Collar in point stitch with crochet edge representing guipure lace, crochet collar imitating Brussels point lace, collar imitating guipure lace.

Constable, Hannah; Clonmel, Ireland; Infants' dress in white thread crochet.

Cross, Mary; Bristol; Crochet counterpane.

Fryer, Miss N.; Barnsley; Crochet counterpane.

Lockwood, Georgiana; London; A child's fancy crochet frock and crocheted toilet cover.

Padwick, Anne; Emsworth; Crochet table cover in Berlin wool, wool toys, tea service.

Thwaites, Mary; Islington; Crochet D'oyleys.

Waterhouse, Emma and Marie; (no town listed); Crochet counterpane in Strutts cotton.

Hooks manufactured for use with fine work produced in the last century and the early part of this century were made to look like those used in tambour embroidery. This tool is shaped like a stiletto with a fine, often very sharp hook on the end. The tension (the evenness of the looped stitches) had to be achieved by making certain that the loop under construction went to exactly the same point along the length of the hook each time. Normally this was achieved by placing a finger on top of the stem of the hook to act as a stop. It also meant that in the earlier days of crochet, one hook could be employed for different tensions and different thicknesses of fine thread just by moving the finger used to create the stop to a different place on the hook.

Throughout this book I have defined crochet as a means of producing a textile using a hook. In order to make anything in crochet it is necessary to have one loop on the hook at all times. No matter how complicated the crochet stitch or pattern construction is, it will start with one loop on the hook and end with one loop on the hook in readiness for the next stage.

When following post-1970 crochet patterns requiring the use of 2.0 mm (size 4) hooks or larger, the loops should be the size of the circumference of the hook's stem. Because hooks manufactured since that date have straight stems with an even diameter throughout, this is an easy rule to follow. Obviously there is shaping near the barbed head and the tension will change if the crochet worker places the loops in that part of the hook instead of on the regular part of the stem.

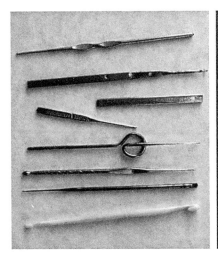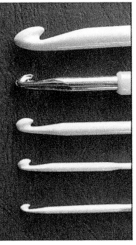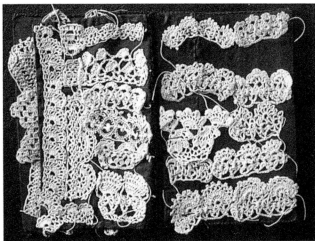

Left: A selection of old crochet hooks. Center: A selection of new crochet hooks. Right: Antique pieces of crochet lace.

Crochet Patterns

Printed crochet patterns did not evolve in a natural way but came into being through consumer demand. The very first patterns were actual samples of crochet that were copied, often working from the crochet sample itself.

Initially the names of the stitches were either translations from European languages or referred to the style of lace that was being copied in crochet. In the beginning the term *crochet en air* was used to distinguish the crochet textile from the hook employed for tambour embroidery, because both involved a tambour style of hook. However, while tambour embroidery produced a design composed entirely of chain stitches that were anchored through a piece of fabric, crochet en air produced chain stitches free from any other material but attached to those chain stitches previously made. This was probably the birth of crochet lace. Assuming that my premise and research findings are correct, this would be the reason why crochet was listed in the embroidery section of the 1851 Great Exhibition catalog. Filet crochet, which is a technique of crochet that copies the needle lace of filet, retained its name, probably because it was the kind of crochet most frequently worked.

During the nineteenth century, information about crochet appeared in needlecraft books by prominent authors such as Mlle Riego and Mrs. Gaugain, to name but two. Mrs. Gaugain called all her crochet work *tambour*; however, all the main writers of

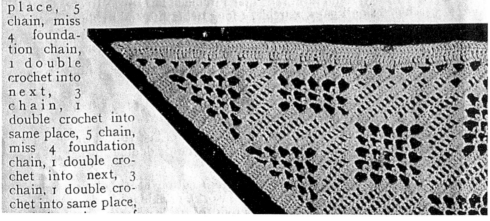

THE "LYDFORD" INSERTION.

Commence with 174 chain.

1st row—1 treble into fourth chain from needle, 1 treble into each of next 4 chain, * 1 chain, miss 1 of foundation chain, 1 treble into next, repeat from * 5 times, 1 treble into each of next 4 chain, ‡ 5 chain miss 3 chain of foundation, 1 double crochet into next, 3 chain, 1 double crochet into same place, 5 chain, miss 4 foundation chain, 1 double crochet into next, 3 chain, 1 double crochet into same place, 5 chain, miss 4 foundation chain, 1 double crochet into next, 3 chain, 1 double crochet into same place,

Old pattern giving lengthy instructions.

the mid-nineteenth century used different terminology for the same process. The lack of consistency in naming crochet stitches and crochet processes persisted for a century. The names of the stitches did not matter until the latter half of the twentieth century because instructions for any design were rarely given—the crochet pattern was either copied from the actual crochet or, in the case of filet crochet, from charts. Books written between 1850 and 1880 with patterns given in words were all accompanied by clear illustrations showing where the stitches lay, usually with a sketch. If you ever get your hands on some of these old patterns, you will find them great fun. Each row or round of instructions constituted an essay, as most writers did not use abbreviations until much later. The secret was and is not to get lost in the reading while trying to follow the instructions.

By the mid-nineteenth century, even though the number of stitches and combination of stitches worked was small, they formed a wide variety of designs. These designs would have small examples kept in fabric books. An actual piece of crochet was worked as a pattern reference and stitched onto either oiled cloth or heavy-duty felt. The book would then become a communal pattern book of crochet designs for a small neighborhood or community. If someone invented a new design by playing around with stitch combinations, they would add a sample to the pattern book for the rest of the neighborhood's inhabitants to copy. At this stage, most crochet designs were lacy, which meant it was easy to copy the flat, open pattern by counting the number of stitches in each row or round.

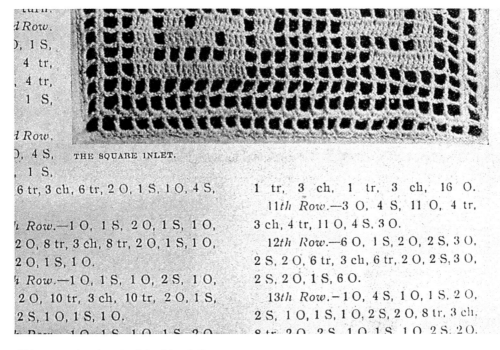

THE SQUARE INLET.

Old pattern showing obsolete abbreviations.

By 1950, the names of the basic stitches printed in patterns within the United Kingdom had been standardized, as had their abbreviations. However, the United States decided to change the naming of their stitches from 1912 until as late as 1936. Until that time, the U.S. used the same terminology as Britain. Now the U.S. names their stitches with the same names but for different techniques. Many designs produced in continental Europe when translated may use either British or American terminology for the names of the stitches. Fortunately, the continental Europe patterns are nearly always accompanied by diagrams using the international crochet symbols. Because you follow symbols and a chart, it does not matter which language the pattern is written in.

Even by 1850, most working-class women could not read and write, although young ladies in the middle and upper classes were becoming accomplished in these tasks. Needlecraft skills were usually learned from governesses, aunts, mothers, or older sisters. Girls were shown how to crochet and copy patterns and not left to read and decipher instructions for themselves. This was an important factor in creating much of the confusion still existing within the craft of crochet. The crochet terminology and the patterns of the post-1950 period still use different names for very similar instructions.

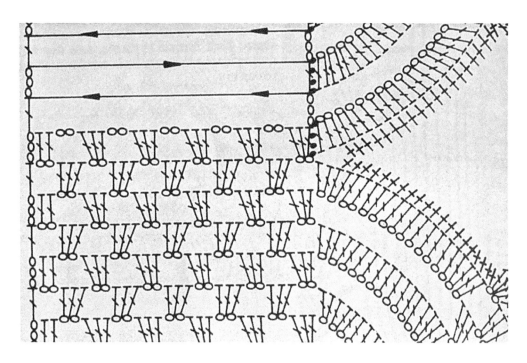

Old pattern showing crochet symbols.

It was not until after 1960 that crocheters began to experiment with different yarns and different ways to insert the hook and genuinely look at the potential of crochet to produce many other techniques. Therfore, throughout the period of 1850 through1950, the stitches remained few and were easily copied. It was only at the end of the twentieth century that people around the world began to want a stable and uniform vocabulary for crochet. Students of crochet were encouraged and inspired to do serious research into crochet as a textile. I am fortunate to house a large number of their findings. The results are ongoing and as more and more people research the subject in a scientific manner, their conclusions continue to amaze. Where some of their findings cover the art of thread crochet, I have included them in this book.

One other aspect of thread crochet that I have observed is the number of times the original lace copies appear in pattern books throughout the world. If you think you have seen a crochet pattern before, the chances are you probably have, either in a different kind of yarn or from another country.

My Conclusions

Summarizing crochet's multifaceted origins, I determined a number of points, which include the following:

A young craft: Crochet is the newest of the textiles using yarn and thread. In recent years it has made a place for itself among the various crafts and art forms, but it has been a struggle.

A pirate craft: Originally, crochet stole its ideas from lace makers and chose to make crochet fabric using implements from other crafts.

Lace imitator: By using an embroiderer's hook and copying lace designs, crochet has made it possible to make a fabric that is similar in looks to lace but made much more quickly. In this way, crochet has become a cheaper version of a much-sought-after trim.

Copying itself: Copies of filet lace designs became prolific, primarily because those who were adept at working with lace thread and a hook were often illiterate. There are many tales of women in service, working on farms or doing other manual work, who went into town on market day, saw a filet-style crochet pattern at a shop, and memorized as much of it as possible. They would crochet this design at home and hope that the shop would not have removed the design they were working on before the following market day.

Home craft: Crochet existed as a home craft long before it became incorporated into fashion or art forms. It is only since the 1970s that various people began to explore the potential of the different techniques required in crochet and to make use of the various combinations of stitches, yarns, hooks and color blending to create new and exciting effects.

Confused history: While searching for proof of the origins of crochet, we can be sidetracked by eminent people informing us that fabrics do not last and that this is why no early samples survive. Often this is to confirm their own belief that crochet is an old textile, despite the fact that fabrics in other media such as weaving, knitting, sprang, and so on can be found.

Art and folklore: Serious researchers will look to folklore and paintings for proof of the existence of a craft or husbandry skill. During the French Revolution, for example, we see paintings of lace making, knitting, weaving, spinning, and even tatting and knotting, but to date no painting of someone working crochet has come to light. Nor are there any known references to crochet in folklore.

Nuns' story: Irish crochet is one of the few branches of crochet that has been well documented because of the efforst of Ursuline nuns, and even here the earliest reference to crochet is at the turn of the nineteenth century when the Ursuline nuns expanded their needlework and included crochet. The first Ursuline convent was formed in 1772 and was well known for its fine needlework. This has led people to believe, erroneously, that the nuns could crochet when the convent was opened.

Chapter One
The Basics

The Basics

There are many ways of exploring the many different facets of crochet, but since this book concentrates on crocheted lace, I have chosen to look at the traditional beginnings as well as the more usual present-day techniques. Should you already be an experienced crocheter, you might like to try out the following instructions, which were originally given in *The Enquirer's Home-Book*, dated 1910. The passage begins with what was required to produce crochet work, and then goes on to tell you how. If you are a beginner to crochet, the following section is for historical interest only; please practice the methods given from page 19 and on first, returning to these more complicated explanations when you feel more proficient.

"...Cotton, thread [presumably linen], wool or silk and a crochet needle are the materials required for crochet work. The long wooden and bone crochet needles are used for wool, while for cotton and silk short steel needles screwed into a bone handle are best. The beauty of crochet work largely depends upon the regularity of the stitches; they must be elastic, but if too loose they look as bad as if too tight. The work should be done only with the point of the needle; the stitch should never be moved up and down the needle.

All crochet work patterns are begun on a foundation chain. There are three kinds of foundation chains. The plain, the double, the purl. The plain foundation consists of chain stitches only.

Plain foundation chain: Form a loop with the cotton or other material with which you work, take it on the needle and hold the cotton, as for knitting, on the forefinger and other fingers of the left hand. The crochet needle is held in the right hand between the thumb and forefinger, as you hold a pen in writing; hold the end of the cotton of the loop between the thumb and forefinger of the left hand, wind the cotton once round the needle by drawing the needle underneath the cotton from left to right, catch the cotton with the hook of the needle and draw it as a loop through the loop already on the needle, which is cast off the needle by this means and forms one chain stitch. The drawing of the cotton through the loop is repeated until the foundation chain has acquired sufficient length. When enough chain stitches have been made, take the foundation chain between the thumb and forefinger of the left hand, so that these fingers are always close to and under the hook of the needle. Each stitch must be loose enough to allow the needle hook to pass easily through. All foundation chains are begun with a loop.

Double foundation chain: Crochet two chain stitches, insert the needle downwards into the left side of the first chain stitch, throw the cotton forward, draw it out as a loop, wind the cotton again round the needle and draw it through the two loops on the needle *draw the cotton as a loop through the left side of the last stitch, wind the cotton round the needle and draw it through both loops on the needle. Repeat from * until the foundation chain is long enough.

Purl foundation chain: Crochet four chain stitches, then one double crochet. In other words, wind the cotton round the needle, insert the needle downwards into the left side of the first of the four chain stitches, wind the cotton round the needle, draw it through the stitch, wind the cotton again round the needle and at the same time draw the cotton through the last loop and through the stitch formed by winding cotton round the needle. Wind the cotton once more round the needle, and draw it through the two remaining loops on the needle. The four chain stitches form a kind of scallop or purl.

The three types of chain. From bottom to top: plain
foundation chain, double foundation chain and purl
foundation chain.

Slip stitch: Draw the needle through the back part of a plain or double foundation chain stitch, or in the course of the work, through the back part of a stitch of the preceding row, wind the cotton round the needle and draw it through the stitch and loop on the needle.

Double stitch: Double stitches are worked nearly like slip stitches. Draw the cotton as a loop through the back part of a stitch, wind the cotton round the needle and draw it through the two loops on the needle.

The ribbed stitch: This stitch is worked backwards and forwards, that is, the right and wrong sides are worked together, which forms the raised ribs. Insert the needle always into the back part of every stitch. Work one chain stitch at the end of every row, which is not worked, however, in the following row…"

It is interesting to see that the double foundation chain and the purl foundation chain are almost nonexistent now. The ribbed stitch reflects the crochet technique of that time by stressing the need to work this stitch in rows rather than in a round or a circle, which was more usual. The British term for this is *single crochet*. Later the use of this variation of a slip stitch as a stitch to form a fabric was rare. However, it is still used to give solidity to all beaded crochet and items such as purses and beaded crochet mats.

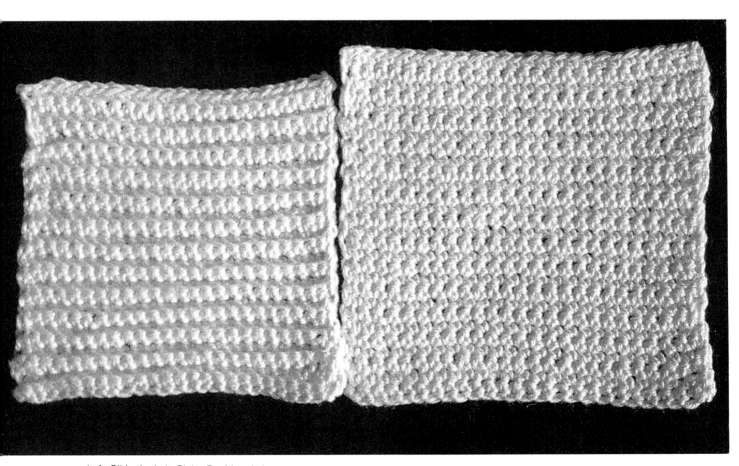

Left: Ribbed stitch. Right: Double stitch.

Twenty-First Century Methods

Since this book focuses on thread or lace crochet, I am concentrating here on the use of the finer threads in cotton, linen, or even silk and fine lurex. Remember, there is no right or wrong way to crochet – only good ways and bad ways. Once you find a method that gives you a high standard of work, stay with it and ignore any well-meaning comments from people who employ a different method.

Hooks

The hooks used for all the stitch patterns and projects in this book are those suitable for finer threads. These hooks are shaped like a stiletto. There are two main ways to hold a crochet hook: like a pencil or like a violin bow. Depending upon where you live, you will hold the hook either as shown above right, which is the way British people tend to hold the hook, or as shown below right, which is the way the majority of people living in Europe hold it. Both ways are commonly used in the U.S. Either way, one of the fingers of the same hand should be used as a stop to prevent the thread loop from sliding farther up the shaped part of the crochet hook.

If you discover that you are gripping the hook too tightly and clenching it rather than letting the hook just lie and flow with your fingers, you might find the hooks with handles easier to manage. Handled hooks are particularly suitable for anyone who is coming to lace crochet after working most of their crochet items in yarn. Equally, hands with stiff joints or other physical problems will find it less of a strain to work with a fine hook that has a handle. Only by experimenting will you know which kind of hook is right for you.

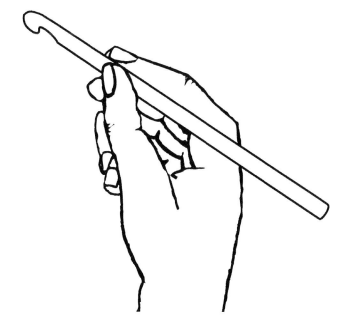

The British preference is to hold the hook like a pen.

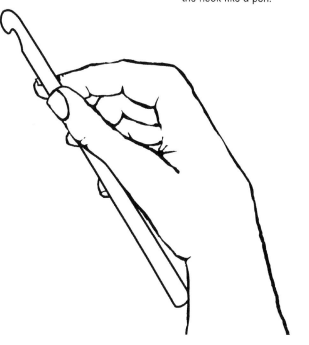

The European preference is to hold the hook like a violin bow.

Threads

If you have crocheted before, please do not change the way you hold your thread. Hold it the way that you are used to, since this will be familiar and make thread crochet much more fun. Only attempt to change how you hold your thread if you are having problems with your tension. Fine cotton and linen threads do not have elasticity incorporated into them during manufacture; therefore, as you hold the thread, it needs to be taut and flow easily through the fingers, without hurting the hand. Yarn, on the other hand, will become thinner if held taut.

There are numerous ways to hold thread or yarn. I find that I do not hold yarn in the same way as thread; I allow it to circle two fingers of my left hand instead of one. When working with thread, however, I find I get a better tension by holding it the more traditional way, which is to wrap it around the little finger once. Be careful you do not grip the thread tightly with the little finger or you could find you have tensed the muscles in your arm right up to your neck. This counteracts the relaxing, therapeutic effect of crochet.

Factors to Consider

Hook type: Choose the hook type carefully (see page 23).

Stitch tension: This should be even, since the lack of elasticity in the thread makes every little deviation noticeable.

Hook size: The size suggested in a pattern may not be the one you need to get the recommended tension. Do not be afraid to change your hook size to achieve the result you need for your project. The chart on page 23 gives recommended hook sizes to use with the different thicknesses of cotton. Use this as a guide only, not a rule.

Varied working methods: As I looked at many patterns over the years and helped others achieve even tension, one very important fact emerged. Not every designer keeps the loops wrapped around the circumference of the hook and holds the hook at a diagonal when working off the loops on the hook (see "Basic Stitches," page 24). Some designers bring the loop through to the front of the work and then lift the hook to a horizontal position to make

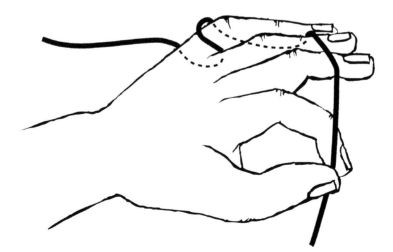

The traditional way of holding thread for crochet.

the stitch longer. This can cause all kinds of difficulties when working in the round, causing what should be a flat motif to either frill or cup. If you have followed the instructions for making the different stitches as given in this book and then come across a pattern in which the designer has elongated the stitch, follow the instructions given in "Motifs," page 57.

Pressing methods: Block pressing makes cotton and linen pieces look better. Pressing for silk or any other fiber (thick or thin) is optional but I would usually advise against it. Crochet has a unique texture and pressing items using any fibers other than cotton and linen can destroy the textured finish.

Mercerized cotton: Most cotton used for lace crochet has an additional finish called mercerization. This is a process that adds luster and prevents fading. A mercerized cotton is difficult, in fact almost impossible, to dye. It is ideal for heirloom crochet.

Stress and tension: You may discover that if you are going through a time of stress, your crochet tension may alter. If this is the case, start another project that is smaller and can be worked on when you are tense. Leave your larger projects for pleasure and leisure—such as while watching TV, listening to the radio, or sitting in the garden on a warm day.

Selecting the Cotton and Hook

The higher the number given to a ball of cotton, the finer it is. Therefore, to purchase a ball of No. 100 cotton is to acquire a thread that is finer than the ordinary, everyday sewing cotton. Without going to a supplier of lace materials, No. 100 cotton is the finest you can purchase for crochet. Other thicknesses are available in No. 80, No. 70, No. 60, No. 50, No. 40, No. 30, No. 20 and No. 10. Some items and fashion designs call for thicker threads such as No. 8, No. 5 and No. 3, but these thicknesses tend not to be mercerized. You may also come across a much-used term *bedspread-weight cotton*. This is equivalent to No. 10 thickness.

When choosing a hook for the thread, the smallest crochet hook available is 0.60 mm (size 14) but you can often get a hook smaller than this from specialist lace suppliers. Another possibility is to scour the antique shops, garage sales, and secondhand stores for the very fine hooks made in the late nineteenth and early twentieth centuries.

When using mercerized cotton threads, linen, or silk for wearable fashion, you will need to increase the hook size to allow the fabric being produced to be softer and to drape well. The chart on page 23 is a generalization of what I recommend. I suggest you try the middle size first to see whether you wish the resulting fabric to be firmer or softer.

Thicker weights can be purchased but often these are used for heavier household, special-effect, and fashion crochet. Some of these cottons will be classed as soft cotton or knitting cotton. To crochet with these heavier weights, look in crochet books dealing with yarn and treat them as yarn rather than thread.

A selection of threads for crochet.

Hook Size for Household Items

Cotton Thickness	Possible Hook Size
100	0.60 mm
80	0.60 mm
70	0.75 mm
60	0.75 mm
50	1.00 mm/0.75 mm
40	1.25 mm/1.00 mm
30	1.25 mm
20	1.50 mm/1.25 mm
10	1.75 mm

Hook Size for Fashion Items

Cotton Thickness	Possible Hook Size
20	2.50 mm/2.00 mm/1.75 mm
10	3.00 mm/2.50 mm/2.00 mm

Crochet threads of different thicknesses

Hook Size for Thick Cotton

Cotton Thickness	Hook Size	
	Household	Fashion
8	1.75 mm	2.50 mm/3.00 mm/3.50 mm
5	2.00 mm/2.50 mm	3.00 mm/3.50 mm/4.00 mm
3	2.50 mm/3.00 mm	3.50 mm/4.00 mm/4.50 mm

Basic Stitches

Having procured thread and a suitable hook, it is time to start crocheting. I suggest you use the largest shaped hook (cotton hook) you can get—a 1.75 mm (size 6) hook – with No. 10 (bedspread-weight) or No. 20 cotton.

It is impossible to crochet unless a loop is on the crochet hook. This loop is there at the beginning of your work and is still there when you come to fasten off, and it is never counted as a stitch. When the loop is first placed on the hook, it is called a slipknot. There are two ways to make a slipknot. In the first method, the tail or short end tightens on the hook and in the second the thread coming from the ball tightens on the hook. I find the first method the most useful, since it enables small motifs and buttons to be made without a central hole. It also has the advantage of hiding the little knot left at the beginning of the work because it can be tightened enough to slide into the first stitch, avoiding any ugly lumps. Occasionally, you may find you prefer to have an immovable knot and to achieve this make the slip knot as shown opposite but substitute "thread from the ball" for "tail end."

Now let's discuss the stitches. There are three basic stitches from which all other stitches and stitch patterns arise. These are the chain, single crochet, and double crochet stitches. The chain does not need to be connected to another type of stitch, while the single crochet attaches itself to other stitches but does not wrap the yarn around the hook before being inserted into the work. The double crochet is the basic stitch that wraps the yarn once around the hook prior to being connected to other stitches. It can be made longer by wrapping yarn around the hook more than once, or shorter by missing one of the processes when removing the loops—this is the half double crochet, which falls between the single crochet and double crochet in length. Basic double crochet is twice as tall as the single crochet and therefore requires more chain to lift the hook to the top of the row.

You will also need to be able to work slip stitches. These are normally used to link a stitch or group of stitches to another point, such as when working in the round, but slip stitches are also used when you want to carry the yarn across a few stitches.

Clusters of stitches can be used to form soft texture. In thread work, you may need as many as five unfinished double crochet in one stitch for the texture to be noticeable. The stitches chosen for the clusters may well be taller than those used to create the row itself, so any turning chain in a row containing clusters should be the number required for the general stitch the row contains. Often clusters are used to work inverted shell patterns when the base of each long double crochet being worked would use a separate stitch in the row below. In this section, the symbols for each crochet stitch are given next to the headings.

Slipknot

1. Place the tail end of the yarn over the main length of yarn to form a loop.

2. Continue wrapping this end over the ball end of the thread and behind the circle you have made.

3. Insert the hook under the single thread that has materialized, as shown in diagram A below.

4. Pull the hook upward to tighten the loop on the hook. At this stage the loop rarely fits snugly on the hook, but a tug with the short end will tighten it to the size required.

Chain (ch)

1. Make a slip knot on the hook. Notice that one side of the length of chain resembles an embroidery chain while the other side resembles a cord. It is the side that looks like embroidery that should face you when working into it.

2. Put the yarn over the hook from back to front as shown in diagram B below.

3. Draw this yarn through the loop already on the hook. You have made 1 chain (ch 1).

4. Continue making chain stitches until you have the required length.

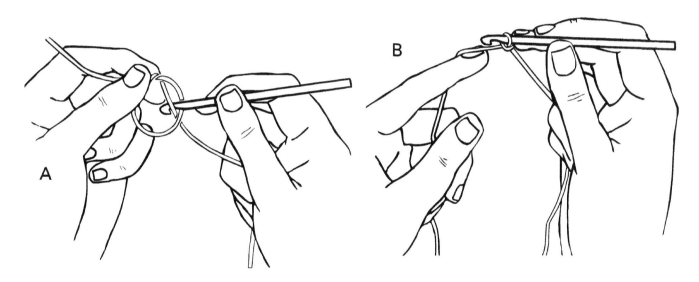

Slip Stitch (ss)

1. Insert the hook into the chain stitch, picking up 2 strands of yarn as shown in diagram A below.

2. Wrap the yarn over the hook (yo) as you did when making a chain. See page 25.

3. Draw the thread through all the loops on the hook. You have made 1 slip stitch (1 ss). A slip stitch can be used to join a length of chain into a ring; see diagram B.

A: Inserting the hook into the chain, picking up two strands of thread.

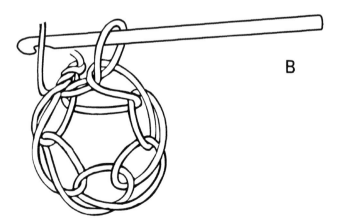

B: Joining a length of chain into a ring with a slip stitch.

Single Crochet (sc)

1. Work a length of chain containing 1 chain for each stitch for the first row plus 1. This is for use as a turning chain.

2. Make sure the smooth side of the chain is facing the front.

3. If you are making a household item, insert the hook from front to back into the third chain from the hook, picking up 1 strand of yarn. Alternatively, if you are making a fashion item, insert the hook from front to back into the third chain from the hook, picking up 2 strands of yarn as shown in diagram C below. Turning chains are counted as the first stitch unless your pattern tells you differently. They are the 2 chains left prior to working the first single crochet.

4. Put the yarn over the hook (yo) and draw through to the front.

5. There are 2 loops on the hook, yo, draw through the 2 loops as shown in diagram D on page 27. Remember, all stitches begin and end with a loop on the hook.

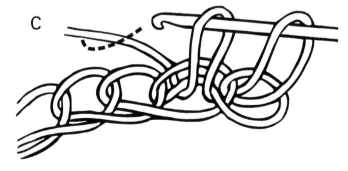

C: Having drawn the thread under two strands, there are two loops on the hook. The thread is in a position to be collected and drawn through both loops.

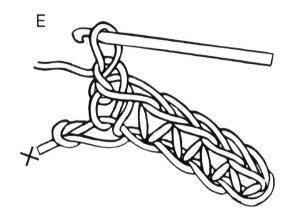

D: The yarn has been drawn through both loops, completing one dc.

6. Although only 1 single crochet has been made, there are 2 stitches completed because of the turning chain. The next single crochet is worked in the next chain, with no chains missed. Continue working 1 single crochet in each chain until all the chains are used. The number of stitches worked should be 1 less than the number of chains you started with, including the turning chain.

7. At the end of the row, chain 1 before turning the work, as shown in diagram E. This is to lift the hook to the top of the next row. You may have noticed that the crochet hook sits on top of the stitches and does not go through the center of them. Therefore, you must lift the hook to that position before commencing the next row or round. Turning chains are the way to achieve this.

8. Turn the work away from you, as shown in diagram F, so that the smooth side of the turning chain will be facing when it is time to make the last stitch at the end of the next row.

9. Insert the hook into the next stitch as shown by the broken line in diagram G. Some patterns call this missing a stitch, but the turning chain is the first stitch and so no stitches have been missed. Continue working 1 single crochet in each stitch to the end of the row. The very last stitch is worked in the turning chain. Repeat the row as many times as desired.

F: The work has been turned and one chain has been made as the first stitch of the row.

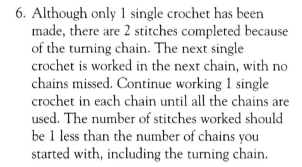

G: The dotted line indicates the point of hook insertion when making the first double crochet, which counts as the second stitch.

Double Crochet (dc)

1. Crochet a length of chain containing as many stitches as are needed for the first row plus 2. This gives you chain 3 to turn—chain 1 for the stitch itself and chain 2 for lift.

2. Place the yarn over the hook (yo).

3. Insert the hook into the fourth chain, as described for making a single crochet, as shown in diagram A.

4. Yo and draw through to the front as shown in diagram B.

5. There are 3 loops on the hook. Yo and draw through 2 loops as shown in diagram C, leaving 2 loops on the hook.

6. Yo and draw through the remaining 2 loops, as shown in diagram D.

7. A double crochet has been made, but there are 2 stitches counting the chain 3 as a stitch. Continue to work 1 double crochet in each stitch to the end without missing any chains. Chain 3 before turning.

8. Turn the work in the direction given for single crochet. Be careful where you place the first double crochet on the next row—the double crochet is longer than a single crochet and the hook is farther away from the point of insertion into the work. Unfortunately, this makes it easier to assume you have missed the place where the turning chain rises and place the first double crochet in the same place. By doing so, you would create an additional stitch and give your work an edge that is slightly wavy and not absolutely straight. To guarantee a straight edge, the first double crochet (second st) goes into the stitch after the turning chain.

9. Continue placing 1 double crochet in each stitch to the end, always picking up the chain top of the stitch in the previous row, which contains 2 strands of thread. When you have worked what appears to be the last stitch, check that you have placed a double crochet in the top of the turning chain.

A

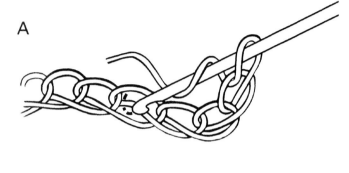

B

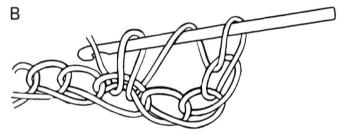

C

D

Half Double Crochet (hdc)

1. Wrap the yarn round the hook and insert into the fourth chain from the hook exactly as if you were making a double crochet. Although you can insert your hook under whichever two strands you choose, you must choose the same two strands of thread for each stitch worked.

2. Yo and draw through to the front, leaving 3 loops on the hook as shown in diagram E.

3. Once again this looks exactly like the double crochet when you start the stitch. Yo and draw through all 3 loops at once, as shown in diagram F, which makes the stitch shorter than a double crochet and is excellent for producing smooth petal shapes and diagonals. Unlike all other stitches, the top of the half double crochet has 3 strands of thread and not 2.

Treble (tr)

1. Wrap the yarn around the hook twice before inserting it into the fifth chain from the hook.

2. Yo and draw through to the front, resulting in 4 loops on the hook as shown in diagram G.

3. (Yo and draw through 2 loops) 3 times to leave 1 loop on the hook.

4. In the first row, sometimes known as the foundation row, work 1 treble in the fifth chain from the hook, and 1 treble in each chain to the end. Chain 4 before turning the work as shown for the single crochet. Continue making rows of treble in the way described for the double crochet.

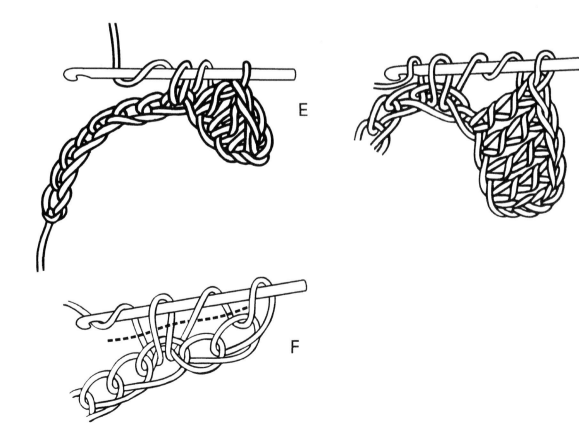

E

G

F

Double Treble (dtr)

1. Wrap the yarn over the hook 3 times.

2. Insert the hook into the sixth chain from the hook in the usual way.

3. Yo and draw through to the front, resulting in 5 loops on the hook as shown in diagram A.

4. (Yo and draw through 2 loops) 4 times to leave 1 loop on the hook.

5. Continue making 1 double treble in each chain to the end. Chain 5 before turning the work. Proceed as for the other treble stitches.

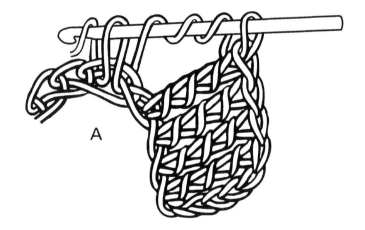

Triple Treble (trtr)

An even longer stitch is obtained by wrapping the yarn over the hook 4 times as shown in diagram B. Insert the hook into the seventh chain from the hook. Remove the loops in twos as described for the other tall trebles.

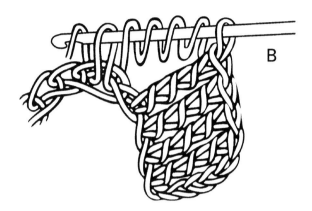

Quadruple Treble (quad)

This stitch is used primarily to give height to certain shapes and to help in forming right angles in some designs. Because it is so tall it is not a good stitch for fabric making. Wrap the yarn over the hook 5 times to give 7 loops on the hook as shown in diagram C. Insert the hook into the eighth chain from the hook. Remove the loops in twos as described for the other tall trebles.

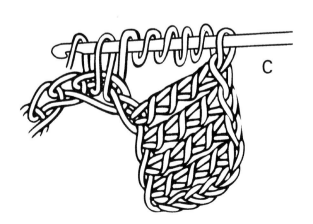

Crab Stitch

A crab stitch is really a single crochet worked backward. In other words, the stitches are worked, with the right side facing, from left to right instead of right to left, assuming you are right handed. No turning chain is required when the crab stitches are worked in the round, but chain 1 is advisable at the beginning of a row to give a crisp corner on a straight edge.

1. Insert the hook into the next stitch on the right, picking up two strands of thread as normal.

2. Drop the hook head onto the thread as shown in diagram D.

3. Bring the thread through to the front of the work, tilting the hook upward to make sure there are 2 loops on the hook; otherwise, you get a backward slip stitch.

4. Twist the hook to a normal working position, yo, and draw through the 2 loops.

Picots

Picots are extensions of making chains that are used extensively in Irish crochet and also in other styles of crochet that copy bobbin and needle lace. To make a picot, work a few chains (usually 3 or 4) and connect them with a slip stitch. This gives a bump and forms a decorative feature within the crochet fabric. It can also be incorporated on the last row of the work as an edging.

E

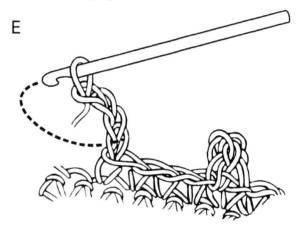

D

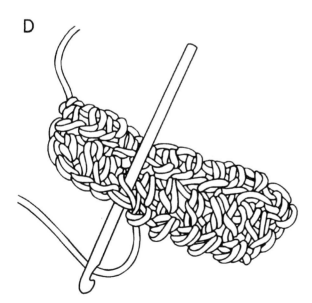

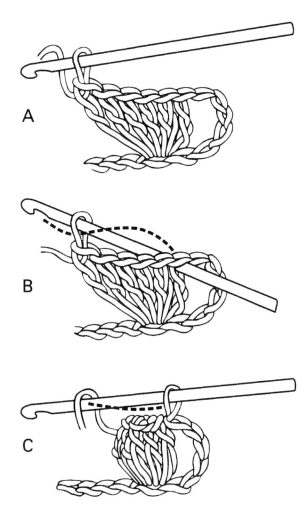

Popcorns

Popcorns are pronounced bumps that are made by working several completed stitches into the same place. These are ideal in thread crochet where the bobbles require extra definition.

With the right side of the crochet facing, work 5 double crochet into the same stitch (see diagram A). Remove the hook from the working loop and insert it from front to back of the first of the 5 double crochet just made (diagram B). Collect the loose loop and draw it through the stitch (diagram C). You may find you wish to put more than 5 double crochet in the popcorn to increase its size or enlarge the texture for emphasis.

Clusters (cl)

Clusters can be used to form soft texture. In thread work, you may need as many as 5 unfinished double crochet in 1 stitch for the texture to be noticeable. In addition, you may find that the stitches chosen for the clusters will be taller than those used to create the row itself, so any turning chain in a row containing clusters should be the number required for the general stitch the row contains. Often clusters are used to work inverted shell patterns when the base of each long double crochet being worked would use a separate stitch in the row below. As an illustration (see diagram D), I have chosen a 3 double crochet cluster (3 dc cl) with all the stitches in the same place.

1. Yo, insert the hook into the stitch, yo and draw through to the front, giving 3 loops on the hook.

2. Yo, draw through 2 loops.

3. *Yo, insert the hook into the same stitch, yo, draw through to the front, yo, draw through 2 loops, rep from * once, leaving 4 loops on the hook.

4. Complete with yo, and draw this yarn through the remaining 4 loops to give 1 chain top to 3 stitches.

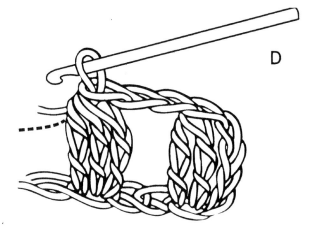

Increasing

Increasing is easy in crochet. Simply work an additional stitch in the same place as the previous stitch—at the beginning of a row you put your hook in the small hole just to the left of the turning chain but before the next stitch. To increase at the end of a row, work 2 stitches in the top of the turning chain of the previous row. This applies to any size of stitch from single crochet, half double crochet, through to quadruple treble. It may be necessary to increase by more than 1 stitch, which would require making an extra chain for the start of the row and using long stitches at the end of a row. (See increasing in filet on page 39.)

Decreasing

1. Work the first stitch as usual until there are 2 loops still left on the hook.

2. Work the second stitch until there are 3 loops on the hook.

3. Yo and draw through all 3 loops. This method of decreasing does not leave holes or create steps. A double crochet decrease described in a pattern is written as dc2tog. (Should you decide to follow one of the older patterns, it will nearly always tell you to slip stitch along to the next stitch at the beginning of the row and to stop before the last stitch at the end of the row. Unfortunately, this gives a stepped effect that prevents you from making pleasing curves. I can only find filet crochet to be the exception to using a stepped increase or decrease. Therefore, I suggest you substitute with the method I have given to obtain a more satisfactory result.)

Fastening Off

1. After working the final stitch, cut the thread from the main ball and leave sufficient length to secure the end neatly by using a sewing needle.

2. Work chain 1 with this end, pulling it straight through the loop so that a little knot is formed.

3. Slide the finger and thumb down this thread so that the knot tightens close to the work.

List of Abbreviations

beg	beginning
blk	block
ch	chain
ch lp	chain loop
ch sp	chain space
cl	cluster
dc	double crochet
dc2tog	decrease 1 double crochet over 2 stitches
dc cl	double crochet cluster
dec	decrease
dtr	double treble
dtr cl	double treble cluster
gr	group
hdc	half double crochet
inc	increase
p	picot
pc	padding cord
quad	quadruple treble
rep	repeat
rnd	round
RS	right side
sc	single crochet
sc2tog	decrease 1 single crochet over 2 stitches
sp	space
ss	slip stitch
st(s)	stitch(es)
tr	treble
tr cl	treble cluster
trtr	triple treble
WS	wrong side
yo	yarn over hook

Hook Size Conversion Chart

International Standard Range (ISR)	U.S. Size
4.50 mm	6/G
4.00 mm	5/F
3.50 mm	4/E 3/D
3.00 mm	2/C/O
2.50 mm	1/B 2 3
2.00 mm	4 5
1.75 mm	6
1.50 mm	7 8
1.25 mm	9 10
1.00 mm	11 12
0.75 mm	13
0.60 mm	14

Chapter Two
Filet Crochet

Filet Crochet

True filet lace is a needle-made lace with a very smooth, flat appearance. When the crochet hook started to copy designs from the needle lace of filet origins, it was impossible to re-create the even look of filet lace—each row of crochet stitches had some twists and lines, creating shadows that were not visible in the needle-lace filet.

When crochet arrived in Britain, the flatter lace designs worked in a continuous piece were the ones most often copied (unlike Ireland, where crocheters tended to copy lace worked in motifs and later assembled). Filet, in particular, with its blocks of solid work and its open spaces in the form of squares, was an easy lace to reproduce. Later, as printed patterns became available in larger quantities, filet crochet was found to be the simplest to describe. It was easy to obtain a clear photographic reproduction and simple to put into chart form. With three ways of presenting the design—samples, charts, or patterns—it was possible for anyone to copy it, no matter how they had been taught to produce crochet work. Because it was very easy to transfer a design idea to graph paper, filet was used extensively for those designs containing words and two-dimensional drawings. It was equally unnecessary for the crochet worker to be able to read. Below is a reference from Rachael Kay Shuttleworth, comparing filet needle lace with a crocheted copy:

> "Filet lace has its beauty in the plain, smooth effect and texture of darning on the netted squares that form a single thread basis with its essential knots at each corner of the mesh. This texture and this effect is unobtainable with a crochet hook and the flat, smooth darned portions are replaced by ridges that form light and shade masses breaking up the surface."

Another objection to crochet copying lace was the coarseness of the thread used, particularly at the end of the nineteenth century and beginning of the twentieth century. No. 100 cotton was readily available but No. 150 cotton was becoming scarce. Using thicker thread was obviously faster but it did remove the delicate tracery effect of the finer laces. Despite the fact that crochet copies were not as aesthetically pleasing as the real laces, it did make lace effects available to a larger number of people.

Around the time of the First World War, filet crochet designs were increasingly abundant for household items and therefore popular with girls to fill their hope chests. Young women, separated from their sweethearts by war, would use the filet crochet technique to crochet messages around the edges of handkerchiefs, which could be carried by the young soldier in his breast pocket. I am the proud owner of a tablecloth depicting implements used in the war, shown below.

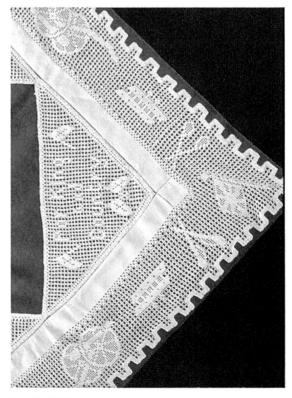

First World War tablecloth, including words, two-dimensional drawings, blocks, spaces, bars, and lacets

Principles of Filet Crochet

The method of working filet crochet has not changed since filet needle lace was first copied in crochet, but the thickness of the thread and how it is used has changed. When working filet crochet, choose a design that shows up clearly. Filet crochet on household linen looks best placed on a contrasting background. Equally, should filet crochet be used for a fashion design, it is important to think of what will be worn underneath the garment, or incorporate a lining in a contrasting color.

Two stitches only are used in the basic squared network of filet crochet. These are chains and double crochet, employed to form either a block or a space. The simplicity of design and uniformity of working the pattern lends itself to graphics. Patterns using international signs and symbols are much easier to follow than those using the written word.

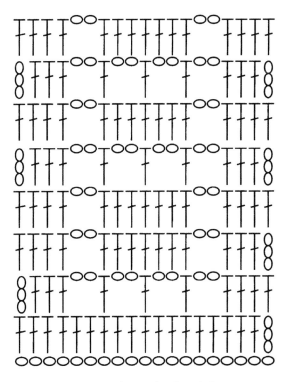

Blocks and spaces using international symbols.

Blocks

Three double crochet form 1 block (blk). When using squared graph paper, the square can be filled in as a solid or marked with a cross or a large dot. Either way, the graph paper indicates that 3 double crochet should be worked for that square. Sometimes you will find that the pattern has not been written out on squared paper but on blank paper. In those instances, you will find 3 double crochet symbols represent the block.

Spaces

Work 2 chains and 1 double crochet for each square of graph paper that is unmarked; this represents a space (sp). On plain paper where international signs and symbols are being used, this will be written as shown next to the heading above.

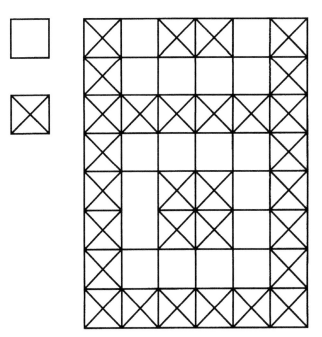

Blocks and spaces on graph paper.

Insertion Strip Design

This simple filet design can be used as an insertion strip. It is worked over 7 squares and has a repeat pattern of 5 rows. Insertion strips are usually incorporated in fabric that has not been crocheted, but they can be used to add interest to articles worked in single crochet or half double crochet. Insertion strips should have both sides worked with a straight edge, making them easier to insert.

Ch 20.

Row 1: 1 dc in eighth ch from hook, 4 sps.

Row 2: Ch 3 (to count as end dc), 2 sps, 1 blk, 2 sps.

Row 3: Ch 3, (1 sp, 1 blk) twice, 1 sp.

Row 4: As row 2.

Row 5: Ch 3, 5 sps.

Rep rows 2–5 to length required.

Working spaces.

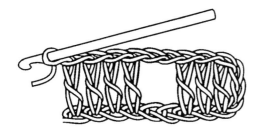

Block, space, block.

Working Filet Crochet

Not all double crochet stitches are worked into the actual stitch. Double crochet stitches placed on top of double crochet stitches are worked as described on page 28—that is, inserting the hook under 2 strands as normal. However, if the double crochet stitches are worked in a space, the hook for the first 2 double crochet should be inserted directly into the space under the chain with the last double crochet being worked into the stitch as usual. Occasionally it may be prudent to work the double crochet stitch directly into each chain of a space, but this does not happen very often.

Most commercial patterns using charts and international signs and symbols give the number of chains required to commence the design and give the first row in words. However, if this is not provided, the following chart will help you calculate the number of chains needed in the foundation chain. It uses the insertion strip design as an example.

Calculating Stitches for Filet Designs	Example	Number	Total
Multiply the number of squares in the chart by	3	7 x 3	21
Add 1 for turning		1	1
Add 2 if starting with a block and going into fourth chain from hook.	2	2	24
*If starting with a space, add another chain 2 and place first double crochet in the eighth chain from hook	2	2	26

*This last line has been added to help you calculate any design that starts with a space rather than a block.

Bars and Lacets

Bars and lacets create a background that is more open than the usual filet designs. On a piece of graph paper, it requires 2 squares in width and 1 square in height for the bar, and 1 square in height for the lacet, making 4 graph squares in all. The lacets are drawn to look like the top of an arch but the bar is unmarked, like the space.

Bar: Work 5 chains and 1 double crochet for 2 squares of graph paper without markings, equaling 6 stitches to make 1 bar. On plain paper where international signs and symbols are being used, it would be written as shown below.

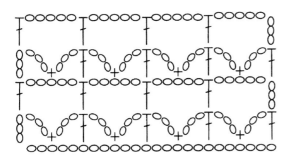

Bars and lacets using international symbols.

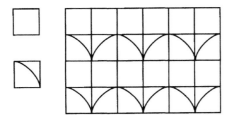

Bars and lacets on graph paper.

Lacet: The lacet completes the design with 3 chains, followed by 1 single crochet worked in the space under the bar, with an additional 3 chains and 1 double crochet worked on top of the double crochet at the end of 2 graph spaces.

Decreasing and Increasing Filet

It is not possible to have a smooth curve when decreasing and increasing in filet, which is why so many patterns have a finishing edge. This is because increases and decreases worked in filet are not achieved stitch by stitch but square by square. If a truly curved edge is required, you must add a final row.

Decreasing at the end of a row: Simply stop one square from the end and turn.

Decreasing at the beginning of a row: Simply slip stitch to the next square and work as normal.

Increasing at the beginning of a row: Add chain to the end of the previous row. For example, add 7 chains for a space and place 1 double crochet in the last stitch of the previous row. For a block, add 5 chains, placing 1 double crochet in the fourth chain from the hook, 1 double crochet in the next chain, and 1 double crochet in the last stitch of the previous row before adding the chain.

Increasing at the end of a row: As the double crochet stitch is quite tall and visible, it is not possible to leave the increasing to the end of a row if the pattern is symmetrical. The shaping must take place at both edges. You need to use long stitches that give the height of a double crochet plus the equivalent chain or chains needed for the block or space.

Adding a Block at the End of a Row

1. The last stitch before adding a block will be a double crochet. Place 1 treble in the same chain as this last double crochet.

2. Work 1 treble in the last crossover strand of the previous treble as shown below.

3. Place 1 double crochet in the last crossover strand of the previous treble to complete the three stitches required for the block.

Notice that the treble bends to the height of a double crochet and provides you with a mock base chain.

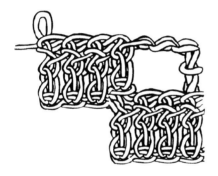

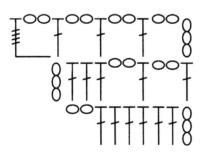

Adding a Space at the End of a Row

1. Chain 2.

2. Work triple treble placed in the same chain as the last double crochet. This bends to give enough length for 3 mock base chains and 1 double crochet. (See diagram 6.)

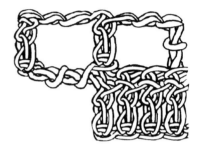

Working Practice

Patterns written for filet do not use the actual stitches. It is assumed that the crocheter knows she must place 3 double crochet for a block (blk) and chain 2, 1 double crochet for a space (sp). Note also that when you work a block after a space it will look as though you have worked 4 double crochet, but the first double crochet belongs to the space and not to the block. Two blocks after 1 space will give you 7 double crochet.

Edgings

Old pattern books are full of very deep edgings worked in filet that were used extensively for tableware and bathroom linen, along with many filet edgings that were narrower to add to lingerie. Yokes for camisoles plus triangular corner insertions were also popular. If you are interested in filet crochet, treat yourself to a look in a secondhand bookstore and see what you can find. There are still many early twentieth-century patterns to be found.

Edgings usually have only one straight edge. The shaped edge can be castellated, scalloped, or in a Van Dyke (chevron) shape. Enjoy trying the four edgings shown on this page and pages 42–45, using the shaping techniques given previously. The first two patterns are both written in words and shown as graphs (the direction in which the rows should be worked is shown in the bottom corner of each graph). No materials have been given. You may work these edgings in any thickness with the corresponding hook. The only difference will be an edge worked in No. 100 cotton and a 0.60 mm (size 14) hook will be considerably smaller than the same edge worked in No. 10 cotton and a 1.75 mm (size 6) hook.

Scalloped Edging with Rose Design

This edging is worked sideways to allow the pattern to be repeated for whatever width is needed.

Ch 87.

Row 1: 1 dc in fourth ch from hook, 11 dc, ch 2, skip 2 ch, 7 dc, (ch 2, skip 2 ch, 1 dc) 3 times, 11 dc, (1 dc, ch 2, skip 2 ch) twice, 13 dc, (ch 2, skip 2 ch, 1 dc) 7 times, 3 dc.

Row 2: Ch 3, 5 sps, 3 blks, 6 sps, 3 blks, 6 sps, 1 blk, 4 sps, ch 5.

Row 3: 1 dc in fourth ch from hook, 2 dc [this is a 1 blk extension], 4 blks, 8 sps, 3 blks, 4 sps, 3 blks, 5 sps, 1 blk.

Row 4: Ch 3, 6 sps, 4 blks, 3 sps, 4 blks, 7 sps, 1 blk, 4 sps, ch 5.

Row 5: 1 dc in fourth ch from hook, 2 dc, 4 blks, 11 sps, 1 blk, 5 sps, 1 blk, 6 sps, 1 blk.

Row 6: Ch 3, 9 sps, 4 blks, 3 sps, 2 blks, 7 sps, 1 blk, 4 sps, ch 5.

Row 7: 1 dc in fourth ch from hook, 2 dc, 4 blks, 7 sps, 2 blks, 1 sp, 3 blks, 2 sps, 3 blks, 2 sps, 4 blks, 1 sp, 1 blk.

Row 8: Ch 3, 3 sps, 5 blks, 1 sp, 2 blks, 1 sp, 2 blks, 2 sps, 1 blk, 1 sp, 2 blks, 7 sps, 1 blk, 4 sps, ch 5.

Row 9: 1 dc in fourth ch from hook, 2 dc, 5 blks, 3 sps, 3 blks, 2 sps, (1 blk, 1 sp) twice, 3 blks, 1 sp, 1 blk, 1 sp, 4 blks, 3 sps, 1 blk.

Row 10: Ch 3, 5 sps, 1 blk, 2 sps, 2 blks, 1 sp, 5 blks, 1 sp, 7 blks, 2 sps, 6 blks, ch 3.

Row 11: 6 blks, 2 sps, 1 blk, 3 sps, 2 blks, 3 sps, 3 blks, 1 sp, 3 blks, 1 sp, 5 blks, 1 sp, 1 blk.

Row 12: Ch 3, 2 sps, 5 blks, 2 sps, 3 blks, 3 sps, 2 blks, 1 sp, 3 blks, 5 sps, 1 blk, 4 sps [1 square reduced].

Row 13: Ch 3, 5 blks, 5 sps, 1 blk, 3 sps, 7 blks, 7 sps, 1 blk, 1 sp, 1 blk.

Row 14: Ch 3, 7 sps, 3 blks, (1 sp, 2 blks) twice, 9 sps, 1 blk, 4 sps.

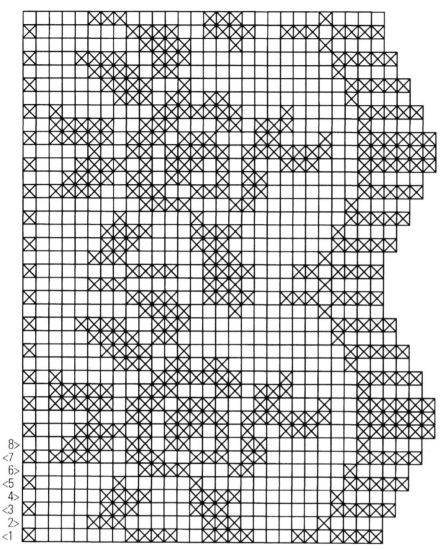

8>
<7
6>
<5
4>
<3
2>
<1

Row 15: Ch 3, 5 blks, 12 sps, 1 blk, 2 sps, 4 blks, 5 sps, 1 blk.

Row 16: Ch 3, 5 sps, 4 blks, 1 sp, 2 blks, 12 sps, 1 blk, 4 sps.

Row 17: Ch 3, 5 blks, 11 sps, 3 blks, 2 sps, 4 blks, 3 sps, 1 blk.

Row 18: Ch 3, 9 sps, 4 blks, 3 sps, 1 blk, 6 sps, 1 blk, 4 sps.

Row 19: Ch 3, 4 blks, 1 sp, 3 blks, (2 sps, 4 blks) twice, 7 sps, 1 blk.

Row 20: Ch 3, 5 sps, (3 blks, 6 sps) twice, 1 blk, 4 sps, ch 5.

Rep rows 3–20 for length required.

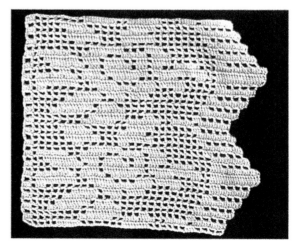

Scalloped edging with rose design.

Van Dyke Edging of Hearts

Ch 39.

Row 1: 1 dc in fourth ch from hook, 2 dc, 2 sps, 5 blks, 3 sps, 1 blk.

Row 2: Ch 3, 3 sps, 5 blks, 2 sps, 1 blk.

Row 3: Ss over 3 sts, ch 3, 1 blk, 2 sps, 3 blks, 1 sp, 1 blk, 1 sp, 1 blk.

Row 4: Ch 3, 2 sps, 4 blks, 2 sps, 1 blk.

Row 5: Ss over 3 sts, ch 3, 1 blk, 2 sps, 2 blks, 2 sps, 1 blk.

Row 6: Ch 3, 6 sps, 1 blk, ch 5 to create a 1-square extension.

Row 7: 1 blk, 2 sps, 2 blks, 2 sps, 1 blk.

Row 8: Ch 3, 2 sps, 4 blks, 2 sps, 1 blk, ch 5.

Row 9: 1 blk, 2 sps, 3 blks, 1 sp, 1 blk, 1 sp, 1 blk.

Row 10: Ch 3, 3 sps, 5 blks, 2 sps, 1 blk, ch 5.

Row 11: 1 blk, 2 sps, 5 blks, 3 sps, 1 blk.

Rep rows 2–11 for length required.

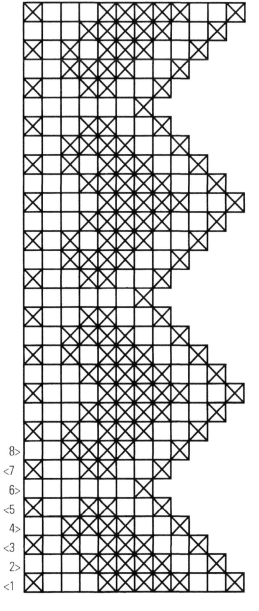

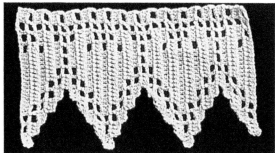

Van Dyke edging of hearts.

Castle Edging

Ch 30.

Row 1: 1 dc in fourth ch from hook, 2 dc, 3 blks, 1 sp, 1 blk, 3 sps. Now follow graph.

Row 2: Ch 3, 1 blk, 1 sp, 3 blks, 3 sps, 1 blk.

Row 3: Ch 3, 4 blks, 1 sp, 1 blk, 3 sps.

Row 4: Ch 3, 1 sp, 1 blk, 3 sps, 1 blk.

Row 5: Ch 3, 2 blks, 1 sp, 3 blks.

Row 6: Ch 3, 1 sp, 1 blk, 3 sps, 1 blk, ch 11.

Rep rows 1–6 for length required.

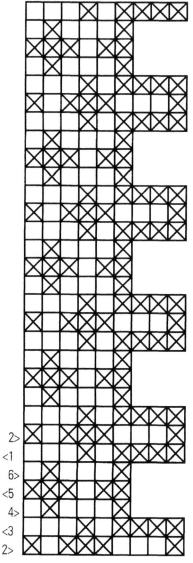

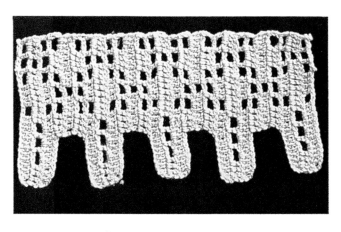

Castle edging

Van Dyke Bricks

Van Dyke or chevron edges are the most common. This version includes bars and lacets.

Ch 63.

Row 1: 1 dc in fourth ch from hook, 5 dc, (ch 3, skip 2 ch, 1 sc in next ch, ch 3, skip 2 ch, 1 dc) twice, 6 dc, ch 2, skip 2 ch, 1 dc, ch 2, skip 2 ch, 7 dc, ch 3, skip 2 ch, 1 sc in next ch, ch 3, skip 2 ch, (1 dc, ch 2, skip 2 ch) 4 times, 7 dc.

Row 2: Ch 3, 6 sps, 1 bar [ch 5, skip the ch 3, 1 sc, ch 3, 1 dc], 2 blks, 2 sps, 2 blks, 2 bars, 2 blks, ch 8 [to create a 2-square extension].

Row 3: 1 dc in fourth ch from hook, 2 dc, 1 blk, 4 lacets, 2 blks, 2 lacets, 4 sps, 2 blks.

Row 4: Ch 3, 6 sps, 2 bars, 2 blks, 4 bars, 2 blks, ch 8.

Row 5: 1 dc in fourth ch from hook, 2 dc, 1 blk, 2 lacets, 2 blks, 4 lacets, 2 blks, 4 sps, 2 blks.

Row 6: Ch 3, 6 sps, 2 blks, 4 bars, 2 blks, 2 bars, 2 blks, ch 8.

Row 7: 1 dc in fourth ch from hook, 2 dc, 1 blk, 2 lacets, 2 blks, 2 sps, 2 blks, 2 lacets, 2 blks, 6 sps, 2 blks.

Row 8: Ch 3, 8 sps, 2 blks, 2 bars, 2 blks, 2 sps, 2 blks, 2 bars, 2 blks.

Row 9: Ss over 7 sts, ch 3, 2 blks, 2 lacets, 2 blks, 2 lacets, 2 blks, 8 sps, 2 blks.

Row 10: Ch 3, 10 sps, 2 blks, 2 bars, 2 blks, 2 bars, 2 blks.

Row 11: Ss over 7 sts, ch 3, 2 blks, 3 lacets, 2 blks, 10 sps, 2 blks.

Row 12: Ch 3, 12 sps, 2 blks, 3 bars, 2 blks.

Row 13: Ss over 7 sts, ch 3, 2 blks, 1 lacet, 2 blks, 6 sps, 2 blks, 4 sps, 2 blks.

Row 14: Ch 3, 6 sps, 2 blks, 6 sps, 2 blks, 1 bar, 2 blks, ch 8.

Row 15: 1 dc in fourth ch from hook, 2 dc, 1 blk, 1 lacet, 2 blks, 6 sps, 2 blks, 1 lacet, 4 sps, 2 blks.

Row 16: Ch 3, 6 sps, 1 bar, 2 blks, 6 sps, 2 blks, 1 bar, 2 blks, ch 8.

Row 17: 1 dc in fourth ch from hook, 2 dc, 1 blk, 1 lacet, 2 blks, 6 sps, 2 blks, 2 lacets, 4 sps, 2 blks.

Row 18: Ch 3, 6 sps, 2 bars, 2 blks, 6 sps, 2 blks, 1 bar, 2 blks, ch 8.

Row 19: 1 dc in fourth ch from hook, 2 dc, 1 blk, 1 lacet, 2 blks, 6 sps, 2 blks, 3 lacets, 4 sps, 2 blks.

Row 20: Ch 3, 6 sps, 3 bars, 2 blks, 6 sps, 2 blks, 1 bar, 2 blks.

Row 21: Ss over 7 sts, ch 3, 2 blks, 6 sps, 2 blks, 4 lacets, 4 sps, 2 blks.

Row 22: Ch 3, 6 sps, 4 bars, 2 blks, 6 sps, 2 blks.

Row 23: Ss over 7 sts, ch 3, 2 blks, 2 sps, 2 blks, 2 lacets, 2 blks, 2 lacets, 4 sps, 2 blks.

Row 24: Ch 3, 6 sps, 2 bars, 2 blks, 2 bars, 2 blks, 2 sps, 2 blks.

Row 25: Ss over 7 sts, ch 3, 2 blks, 2 lacets, 2 blks, 2 sps, 2 blks, 1 lacet, 4 sps, 2 blks.

Row 26: Ch 3, 6 sps, 1 bar, 2 blks, 2 sps, 2 blks, 2 bars, 2 blks.

Rep rows 3–26.

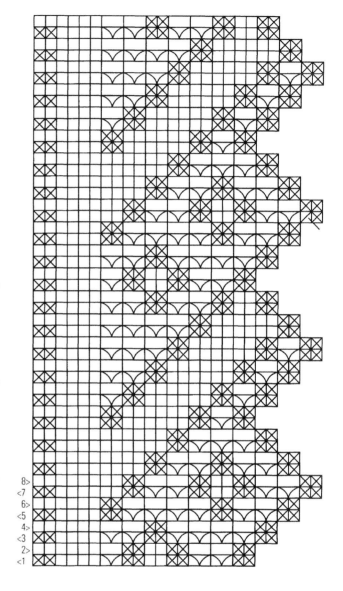

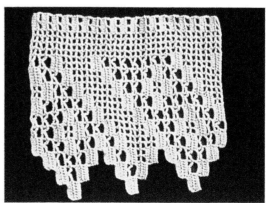

Van Dyke bricks.

Projects

Here are two filet crochet projects for you to try, both of which are fairly straightforward. I have suggested a use for each design, but you could, of course, adapt either of them for other purposes if desired.

Swan Wall Hanging

Try this simple swan design either as a hanging or for the top of a blind. It is worked from the left-hand side of the picture to the right.

The chart begins on page 47 and continues on page 48.

Materials:

• 2 x 75 g balls (approx. 675 yds.) of No. 10 weight thread

• 1.75 mm (size 6) crochet hook

• 1 rod 60 cm (24") long, or to fit window or wall

Size: When finished and measured flat, this project measures 25 cm (10") deep x 52 cm (20½") wide. If you require a longer drop, add additional spaces between the points where the slits for the rod have been worked and the actual pattern.

Ch 132.

Row 1: 1 dc in fourth ch from hook, 2 dc, (1 sp, 1 blk) 21 times [43 squares].

Row 2: Ch 3, 40 sps, 1 blk, 1 sp, 1 blk.

Row 3: Ch 3, 1 blk, 1 sp, 1 blk, 7 sps, 1 blk, 32 sps.

Row 4: (With split) ch 3, 2 sps, ch 15, skip 5 sps anchoring last sp with 1 dc, 24 sps, 3 blks, 6 sps, 1 blk, 1 sp, 1 blk.

Subsequent rows: Follow chart, working 1 blk for each square containing a cross, 1 sp for each unmarked square, and working the split for the unconnected squares that give a long space, as in row 4. See chart opposite.

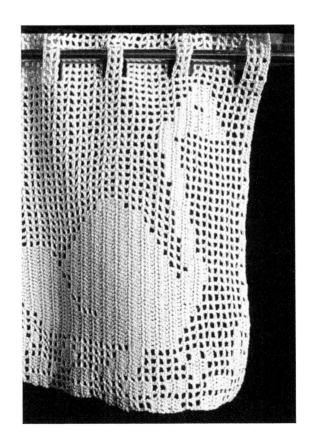

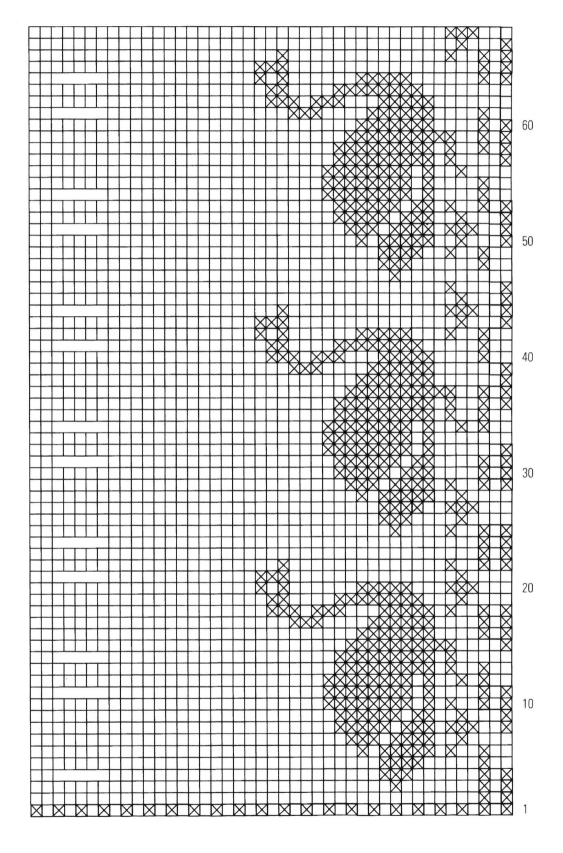

60

50

40

30

20

10

1

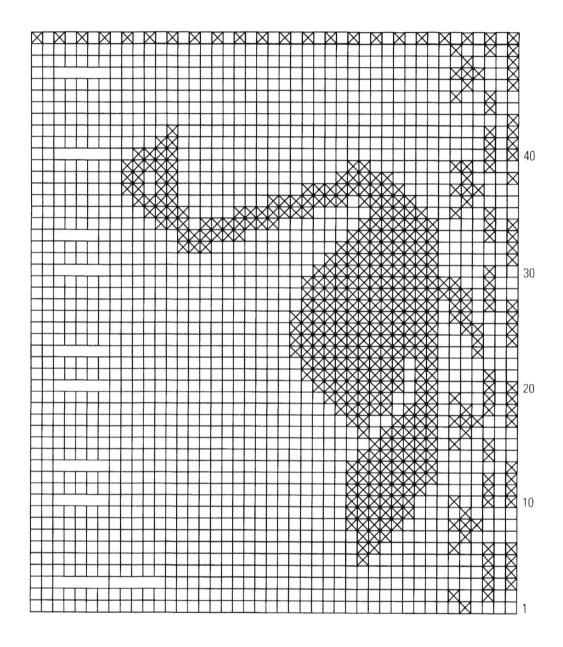

40

30

20

10

1

The finished swan wall hanging.

Diamond Shrug

Here is another simple but effective filet design, this time incorporating shaping. The building bricks of diamond shapes lend themselves to a design based on a diamond. In this instance the diamond is worked from the handkerchief sleeve edge to the opposite sleeve edge and incorporates a cutout from the design to allow it to fit snugly around the neck. Details on increasing and decreasing filet are given on pages 39–40.

Materials:

• 5 x 50 g balls (approx. 1125 yds.) of No. 10 cotton

• 1.75 mm (size 6) crochet hook

Size: From sleeve point to center back 48 cm (19"), center back 57 cm (22½")

Gauge: 1 diamond with sts stroked from bottom to top is 5.7 cm (2¼") wide x 5 cm (2") high.

Ch 6.

Row 1: 1 dc in fourth ch from the hook, 2 dc.

Row 2: Inc 1 square [in readiness for a blk], 3 blks.

Row 3: Inc 1 square [in readiness for a blk], 2 blks, 1 sp, 2 blks.

Row 4: Inc 1 square [in readiness for a blk], 2 blks, 3 sp, 2 blks.

Row 5: Inc 1 square [in readiness for a sp], 2 sps, 2 blks, 1 sp, 2 blks, 2 sps.

Row 6: Inc 1 square [in readiness for a sp], 4 sps, 3 blks, 4 sps.

Row 7: Inc 1 square [in readiness for a sp], 2 sps, 1 blk, 3 sps, 1 blk, 3 sps, 1 blk, 2 sps.

Row 8: Inc 1 square [in readiness for a sp], 2 sps, 3 blks, 5 sps, 3 blks, 2 sps.

Row 9: Inc 1 square [in readiness for a blk], 1 blk (3 sps, 1 blk) 4 times.

Continue following the chart and inc until 143 squares have been made and 9 diamond patterns completed.

Divide for the Neck and Back

Work the next row as pattern, increasing as normal but stopping after 70 squares [including the first inc square] have been completed. Work 7 rows as pattern, inc at the shaped edge but keeping the neck edge straight. Work 8 more rows as pattern, keeping the neck edge straight but then dec at the shaped edge.

Second Side

Ch 229 [225 for squares + ch 2 for turning + ch 2 for sp]. Work the second side to correspond with the first side, continuing the dec at both ends until 1 square is reached.

To Complete

Rejoin the yarn to 1 of the front points. Work 1 sc in each st up to neck, 3 sc over 2 rows across back neck, 1 sc in each st down second front. Fasten off.

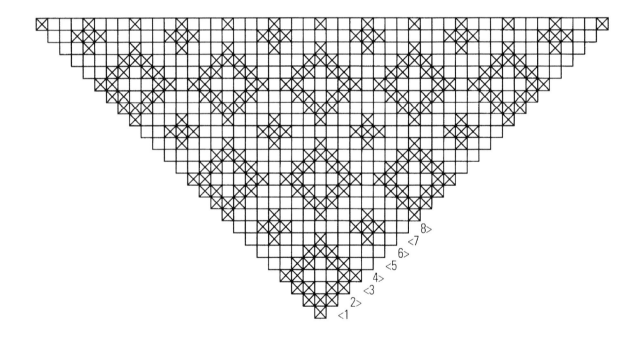

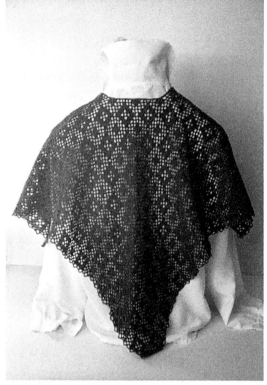

The finished diamond shrug.

Chapter Three
Motifs

Motifs

This chapter looks at the types of motifs that start from the inside and work outward by increase methods to form a complete shape. When you hear someone refer to a motif in crochet, the chances are they are talking about a design begun in this way, although there is another way of working, as you will see in chapter 5. The theme of this book is to look at the origins of lace crochet first, and therefore I could not resist including the following pattern from Volume III of the *Selected Works of Mlle Riego on Crochet, Knitting, Lace Work* by Mrs. Rivers Turnbull. This is a challenge to anyone who enjoys crochet. Not only is the square shamrock motif complex to produce but the way it was originally written is equally challenging. You will find the pattern for this motif repeated on page 60 using the terminology of today. Here is the original.

"Commence with 10 chain. Make it round by working 1 single in the first stitch.

Rnd 1: Work 16 plain in the foundation round, then 1 single in the first stitch.

Rnd 2: 5 chain, miss 1, 1 plain, 8 chain, miss 1, 1 plain. Repeat three more times.

Rnd 3: 3 plain in the 5 chain and for the first oeillet, 8 chain, turn, miss 7, 1 single in the first stitch of the 8 chain, then 1 chain to cross, and in this round loop work 10 plain; 1 single on the 1 chain that crosses, and in the same 5 chain of the second round as before, work 3 plain, then miss 1, and work 5 plain in the 8 chain.

First shamrock: 16 chain; turn, miss 7, 1 single in the eighth stitch of it, leaving 8 chain, turn, 3 chain, 2 long in the round loop, join to the sixth stitch of the 10 plain of the oeillet; then in the round loop, 1 long, 3 chain, 1 single, (3 chain, 3 long, 3 chain, and 1 single, twice), 4 plain on the stem, leaving 4 chain; then 12 chain for the second shamrock.

Second shamrock: Turn, miss 7, 1 single; turn, 3 chain, join to the last long stitch of the first shamrock, then in the round loop, 3 long, 3 chain, 1 single, (3 chain, 3 long, 3 chain, and 1 single, twice), 4 plain on the stem, then 12 chain for the third shamrock.

Third shamrock: Same as second; when finished, work 4 plain down the center stem, then 5 plain in the same 8 chain of the second round as before; miss 1, 3 plain in the 5 chain.

Second oeillet: 8 chain, turn, miss 7, 1 single, turn, 1 chain to cross, 4 plain in the round loop, join to the center long stitch of the last shamrock, then 6 plain in the round loop, 1 single and 3 plain in the same 5 chain as before; miss 1, 5 plain in the 8 chain. Repeat from the first shamrock three times more; but in the last pattern only work to the 5 plain in italics, as the oeillet will not be required. Then work 7 single on the first stitches of the round and up the first oeillet; join to the last long stitch but one of the last shamrock, 1 single on the oeillet, and fasten off.

Work 31 more diamonds the same; this will make an ordinary full-sized couvrette."

Motifs for Today

Many shapes can be started in the center, and perhaps the most common of these is the much-used, often-seen granny square, worked in scraps of leftover yarn for lap-size and large blankets. (Details on how to work a granny square are given on page 59.)

Circles, squares, triangles and so on can all start from a central point. Assuming that the designer and the crocheter work in a similar way, the completed motif will be flat. There are certain simple mathematical formulas that you need to know, particularly if you wish to design motifs for yourself or are trying to work out why one motif cups, another frills, and the rest remain flat. These are given in the chart on page 56. The points listed below should help.

Base: The base of a stitch can be drawn in and gathered, while the top or chain finish of a stitch cannot. The motif would be cup-shaped if the top of the stitch was gathered.

Circumference: The stitch determines the circumference of a circle, not the base, so when confirming that a motif is lying flat, always look at the outer edge.

Increases: The number of increases per round depend on the height of the stitch you are using. For instance, a round of single crochet requires 6 increases, while a round of double treble needs 24.

Even circles: To produce a perfect circle, avoid increasing in the same place on every round. If you do increase in the same place on each round, you will find you are creating points with straight lines between them, producing shapes such as a hexagon or an octagon.

Other shapes: A circle can be changed into various shapes, such as a triangle, square, hexagon, or octagon, by varying the points of increase, and sometimes also the number of increases placed at each point.

Height adjustment: When the stitch height is changed within a pattern design, the number of increases should also be changed.

Markers: Place a piece of contrast thread or a marker at the join so that you can see exactly where the round starts.

Slip stitch join: I have found that I produce the best work if I join each round with a slip stitch, make my turning chain to lift the hook, and then turn the work. By going backward and forward as though working in straight rows, there seem to be fewer problems with walking seams than if the front of the work is facing all the time.

Alternative join: Occasionally the join may not look very nice. Instead of a slip stitch, you can remove the hook from the loop and insert it into the stitch where there would normally be a slip stitch. The hook can be inserted front to back or back to front. Collect the loop and complete the round by using the loose loop as a slip stitch. You will have to observe which way to insert the hook to make the neatest join for each individual design.

Hook insertion: Since most motifs are worked with the right side facing, the hook should be inserted to the right of the stem of the stitch, unlike working in rows when the hook is inserted into the left-hand side of a stitch. (Left-handed crocheters must reverse these instructions.)

Fastening the ends: Because it is not easy to fasten in the ends of thread, it is advisable to work over the starting end with the first few stitches made while working the first round.

Number of Increases for Different Stitch Heights

Procedure	Single Crochet	Half Double Crochet	Double Crochet	Treble
Start with	ch 4	ch 4	ch 4	ch 5
Join with	1 ss	1 ss	1 ss	1 ss
Make	ch 1	ch 2	ch 3	ch 4
Place stitches in the center of ring	5 sc	7 hdc	11 dc	23 tr
Join with	1 ss	1 ss	1 ss	1 ss
Make	ch 1	ch 2	ch 3	ch 4
Turn work, place 1 st in the same place	2 sc in each st	2 hdc in each st	2 dc in each st	2 tr in each st
This has given an inc per round of	6 sc	8 hdc	12 dc	24 tr
Continue to inc on each round by	6 sc	8 hdc	12 dc	24 tr
The inc even after 50 rounds should be the same as for round 2, which is	6 sc	8 hdc	12 dc	24 tr

Shapes

Triangles: To change the circle into a triangle, divide the number of increases per round and place them in 3 places only. For single crochet, that means 2 additional stitches, making 3 single crochet in 1 stitch (1 stitch acting as the original stitch plus 2 extra stitches for the increasing). For treble there would be as many as 8 additional stitches in 3 places to give 9 treble in the same place. This may require a pattern adjustment in a lacy design.

Squares: To make a square, the increases should be divided into 4; therefore in single crochet, which has 12 increases over 2 rounds, it would mean increasing on every other round.

Hexagons: These are easy to design for single crochet. Instead of staggering the point of increase to shape the motif into a circle, increase in the same place each time and a hexagon will emerge. With other stitches, it means putting more than one extra stitch into the increase points. The number of extra stitches will depend upon how tall the stitch is.

Octagons: These are formed quickly when using half double crochet and the same principle as above applies. You must increase at eight points. With other stitch heights you may find you have to omit increases on occasional rounds to keep the design flat.

Semicircles: These are a challenge, particularly if you are trying to keep a straight edge along the line of the diameter. In crochet, the stitches want to gather at their base and spread widthways at their head. In a semicircle, there is no natural balance created by stitches in the other half of the circle; therefore, there is no opposing pull to make the stitches conform.

Different Working Methods

As already discussed, not everyone is taught to crochet in the same way. In fact, some people are not taught to crochet at all but to simply find their own way through experimentation. However, the majority of today's written instructions and the teachers of crochet around the world use the methods described in chapter 1. I will call this method 1 (see diagram A). However, there are other ways of executing the stitches that will result in a common stitch such as the double crochet being lengthened. Here I will focus on the three ways a stitch can be worked, using the double crochet as an example. It will be up to you to adapt any other stitch you may come across if it is not producing the size or tension you require.

Eastern Europeans have a tendency to insert the hook into the stitch, bring it through to the front of the work and make one chain in the first loop on the hook. They do this extra step before removing the remainder of the loops in twos. This is method 2.

The third method changes the height of the stitch by the way the wrist moves. The hook is not kept at an angle but flicked up by the wrist into a horizontal position, lengthening the loop from the base of the stitch to the first diagonal cross bar (see diagram B).

A

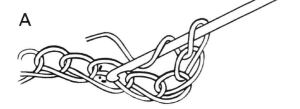

Treble worked with the hook at an angle (method 1).

B

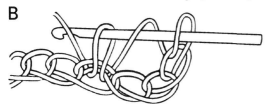

Treble with the hook held horizontally (method 3).

As I commented earlier, when working a motif from the center it is the outer edge that determines how many increases are required to keep the motif flat. If a designer uses either method 2 or 3, the stitch will be longer than if worked by method 1. This means there must be more increases in each round than given for that stitch in the table. Method 2 tends to make it the height of a treble and therefore the guideline for trebles should be followed.

Troubleshooting

Center buckles: If only the central section of a motif buckles, (which often occurs when the pattern changes from a dense or close fabric to a more lacy pattern), check that the chains in the lacy section are not either too tight (causing it to cup) or too loose (creating frilling). You may find that by changing your hook size for the central section and returning to the recommended hook size for the lacy part, you can rectify the situation.

Frilly all over: If the whole motif becomes frilly instead of lying flat, it indicates that the outer edge is too large for the design. There are three possible ways to correct frilling:
1. Include fewer increases per round (if the pattern allows for this adjustment).
2. Use a larger crochet hook for the pattern.
3. Elongate the stitches so that the circumference is further away from the center of the circle by adopting either method 2 or method 3.

Bowl shape: If the pattern has become bowl-shaped, try the following:
1. Check if the stitches are being accidentally lengthened at the point of insertion and, if so, adjust them accordingly.
2. Check that the stitches are not too tight and alter accordingly.
3. Include more increases in each round (as long as the pattern allows for this).

Library of Motifs

Here are 12 motifs for you to try. I have used asterisks to mark the degree of difficulty of a pattern. One asterisk indicates that the pattern is easy, two show that it requires a little more thought, and three asterisks are given when the motif is challenging. The shamrock square from Mlle Riego has four asterisks!

Small Popcorn Octagon **

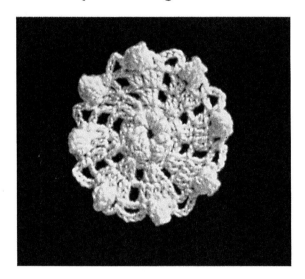

Ch 8, join with 1 ss to form a ring.

Rnd 1: This rnd is WS of motif. Ch 1, (1 tr, 1 sc into ring) 5 times, 1 tr, join with 1 ss to top of turning ch, turn.

Rnd 2: Work with RS facing. Ch 1, 1 sc in same place, *2 sc in next sc, rep from * 6 times, join with 1 ss to top of turning ch.

Rnd 3: Ch 3, skip 1 st, *1 sc in next st, ch 2, skip 1 st, rep from * 6 times, join with 1 ss to top of turning ch.

Rnd 4: Ch 3, 2 dc in same place, *ch 2, 3 dc in next sc, rep from * 6 times, ch 2, join with 1 ss to top of turning ch.

Rnd 5: Ch 3, 1 dc in same place, 1 dc on next dc, 2 dc in next dc, *ch 2, 2 dc in next dc, 1 dc, 2 dc in next dc, rep from * 6 times, ch 2, join with 1 ss to top of turning ch.

Rnd 6: Ch 4, one 6-dc popcorn in central dc, ch 3, skip 1 st, 1 sc in next st, * ch 5, skip 2 ch, 1 sc in next st, skip 1 st, ch 3, 1 popcorn in next st, ch 3, skip 1 st, 1 sc in next st, rep from * 6 times, ch 5, join with 1 ss to first ch of ch 4.

Hexagon Star **

Ch 4, join with 1 ss to form a ring.

Rnd 1: Ch 1, 5 sc in center of ring, join with 1 ss to turning ch.

Rnd 2: Ch 3, 2 dc in same st, (ch 3, 3 dc in next st) 5 times, ch 3, join with 1 ss to top of turning ch.

Rnd 3: Ch 3, dc2tog over next 2 sts, *ch 6, skip 3 ch, dc3tog over next 3 sts, rep from * 4 times, ch 6, join with 1 ss to top of turning ch.

Rnd 4: Ch 6, 1 dc in same place, *ch 5, 1 sc worked under ch 3 of rnd 2, ch 5, (1 dc, ch 2, 1 dc) in center of cluster, rep from * 4 times, ch 5, 1 sc worked under ch 3 of rnd 2, ch 5, join with 1 ss to third ch of ch 6.

Rnd 5: Ch 4, (1 dc, ch 1, 1 dc) in same cluster, *ch 2, 1 ss on sc, ch 2 (1 dc, ch 1 in next cluster) twice, 1 dc in same cluster, rep from * 4 times, ch 2, 1 ss in sc, ch 2, 1 ss in third ch of ch 4. Fasten off.

Basic Wheel **

If your chains are tight, add 1 or 2 more when working this design. This simple wheel motif will only cup if your ring is too small.

Ch 12, join with 1 ss to form a ring.

Rnd 1: Ch 5, 1 tr in center of ring, *ch 2, 2 tr in ring, rep from * 10 times, ch 2, join with 1 ss to top of turning ch.

Rnd 2: Ss to ch-2 sp, ch 3, 3 dc cl in same space to form a cluster, *ch 7, 4 dc cluster in ch-2 sp, rep from * 10 times, ch 4, 1 tr in top of 3 dc cluster.

Rnd 3: Ss to center of ch-7 sp, (ch 8, 1 sc in ch-8 sp) 11 times, 1 ss to join. Fasten off.

Granny Square *

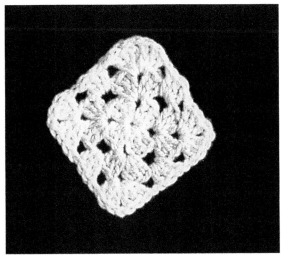

This motif was incorporated into designs so much during the 1970s and 1980s that it began to look dated, and discriminating designers began to avoid it. However, the motif can look extremely effective in white and a deep ecru thread, as well as if it is worked using two contrasting colors.

Ch 4 with main-color thread, join with 1 ss to form a ring.

Rnd 1: Ch 3, 2 dc into ring, *ch 1, 3 dc into ring, rep from * twice, ch 1, join with 1 ss to top of turning ch. Break off yarn.

Rnd 2: Join contrast thread to any ch sp. Ch 3, (2 dc, ch 1, 3 dc) in same sp, ch 1, *(3 dc, ch 1, 3 dc) in next ch sp, ch 1, rep from * twice, join with 1 ss to top of turning ch. Break off yarn.

Rnd 3: Join main thread to any sp between corner groups. Ch 3, 2 dc in same sp, *ch 1, (3 dc, ch 1, 3 dc) in next ch sp [for corner], ch 1, 3 dc in next ch sp, rep from * twice, ch 1, (3 dc, ch 1, 3 dc) in next ch sp, ch 1, join with 1 ss to top of turning ch.

Shamrock Square ****

Although shamrocks are frequently associated with Irish crochet, this square is not made in the Irish way, starting with the motifs and then forming them into an article, which is why I have included it in this section.

Ch 10, join with 1 ss to form a ring.

Rnd 1: Ch 1, 15 sc in center of ring, join with 1 ss to top of turning ch.

Rnd 2: *Ch 5, skip 1 st, 1 sc, ch 8, skip 1 st, 1 sc in next st, rep from * 3 times.

Rnd 3: Incorporate all 4 corner shamrocks of the square, 3 sc in ch-5 sp, *ch 8, 1 sc in eighth ch from hook to form a loop, ch 1, turn. Work 10 sc in loop, 1 ss to join the sc sts into a ring, 3 sc in same ch-5 sp of rnd 2 as first sc worked in rnd 3, 5 sc in ch-8 sp.

Continue for first shamrock of first corner with ch 16, 1 ss in eighth ch from hook, [leaves 8 ch], turn, ch 2, 2 dc in ring just made, join to sixth sc of 10 sc in loop, 1 dc, ch 3 to complete the first leaf of first shamrock; 1 ss in ring, (ch 2, 3 dc, ch 3, 1 ss in same ring) twice, 1 sc in next 4 ch to

form stem, [leaves 4 ch], ch 12 for second shamrock of first corner, 1 ss in eighth ch from hook; turn, ch 2, join to last dc of first shamrock, (3 dc, ch 2, 1 ss) in ring just formed, (ch 2, 3 dc, ch 2, 1 ss in same ring) twice, 1 sc in next 4 ch to form stem, ch 12 for third shamrock of first corner. Work as for second shamrock of first corner including short stem, 1 sc in rem 4 ch of first ch 16 made for first shamrock, 5 sc to complete ch-8 sp of rnd 2, 3 sc in ch-5 sp, rep from * 3 times for next 3 corners of square.

Dahlia Circle **

This striking dahlia design is fairly easy to create, and it would look great framed or used as a table mat.

Ch 5, join with 1 ss to form a ring.

Rnd 1: Ch 1, 5 sc in ring, join with 1 ss to top of turning ch.

Rnd 2: Ch 1, 1 sc in same place, 2 sc in each st to end, join with 1 ss to top of turning ch.

Rnd 3: Ch 1, 1 sc in same place, *ch 1, skip 1 st, 2 sc in next st, rep from * 4 times, ch 1, join with 1 ss to top of turning ch [18 sts].

Rnd 4: Ch 1, 1 sc, *2 sc in ch sp, 2 sc, rep from * 4 times, 2 sc in ch sp, join with 1 ss to top of turning ch.

Rnd 5: Ch 3, * 4 sc, ch 1, rep from * 4 times, 3 sc, join with 1 ss to top of turning ch [30 sts].

Rnd 6: Ch 1, *2 sc in ch sp, 4 sc, rep from * 5 times, join with 1 ss to top of turning ch.

Rnd 7: Ch 3, 1 dc, *ch 2, skip 1 st, 2 dc, rep from * 10 times, ch 2, join with 1 ss to top of turning ch.

Rnd 8: Ch 3, 2 dc in next st, *ch 2, skip 2 ch, 1 dc, 2 dc in next st, rep from * 10 times, ch 2, join with 1 ss to top of turning ch.

Rnd 9: Ch 3, 1 dc, 2 dc in next st, *ch 2, skip 2 ch, 2 dc, 2 dc in next st, rep from * 10 times, ch 2, join with 1 ss to top of turning ch.

Rnd 10: Ch 3, 2 dc, 2 dc in next st, *ch 2, skip 2 ch, 3 dc, 2 dc in next st, rep from * 10 times, ch 2, join with 1 ss to top of turning ch.

Rnd 11: Ch 3, 3 dc, 2 dc in next st, *ch 2, skip 2 ch, 4 dc, 2 dc in next st, rep from * 10 times, ch 2, join with 1 ss to top of turning ch.

Rnd 12: Ss to next st, ch 3, 4 dc, *ch 5, skip 2 ch and 1 dc, 5 dc, rep from * 10 times, ch 5, join with 1 ss to top of turning ch.

Rnd 13: Ss to next st, ch 3, 3 dc, *ch 3, 1 dc in ch-5 sp, ch 3, skip 1 st, 4 dc, rep from * 10 times, ch 3, 1 dc in ch-5 sp, ch 3, join with 1 ss to top of turning ch.

Rnd 14: Ss to next st, ch 3, 2 dc, *ch 3, (1 dc in ch-3 sp, ch 3) twice, skip 1 st, 3 dc, rep from * 10 times, ch 3, (1 dc in ch-3 sp, ch 3) twice, join with 1 ss to top of turning ch.

Rnd 15: Ss to next st, ch 3, 1 dc, *ch 3, (1 dc in ch-3 sp, ch 3) 3 times, skip 1 st, 2 dc, rep from * 10 times, ch 3, (1 dc in ch-3 sp, ch 3) 3 times, join with 1 ss to top of turning ch.

Rnd 16: *1 sc in center of 2 dc, (3 sc in next ch sp, skip 1 dc) 3 times, 3 sc in ch-3 sp, rep from * to end, join with 1 ss. Fasten off the thread.

Optional row: If desired, you can add a final row of 5 sc, 1 picot.

Paddle Stitch *

This attractive motif can, if desired, be extended to form much larger paddle motifs, thereby reducing the number of motif connections required.

Ch 9 and join with 1 ss to form a ring.

Rnd 1: 16 sc into ring, ss into first sc.

Rnd 2: 1 sc into same place as ss, *(ch 5, skip 1 sc, 1 sc) into next sc, rep from * ending with ch 5, 1 ss into first sc.

Rnd 3: *Ch 4, 2 sc into next ch-5 sp, 1 sc into next sc, rep from * around.

Rnds 4–15: *Ch 4, 2 sc into next ch-4 sp, 1 sc in each sc of sc group except skip last sc of group, rep from * around. (On last rnd, you will have 15 sc in each sc group.)

Rnd 16: *Ch 4, 1 sc into next ch-4 sp, skip next sc, 1 sc in each of next 13 sc, skip last sc, rep from * around.

Rnd 17: *(Ch 5, 1 sc into next loop) twice, ch 5, skip next sc, 1 sc in each of next 11 sc, skip last sc, rep from * around.

Continue in this manner, working 2 less sc (the first and last sc) in each sc group, and 1 more loop between sc groups on each rnd until 1 sc remains in each sc group, end with ss in last ch of ch-5 loop, and ss into first sc.

Medallion **

Ch 6, join with 1 ss to form a ring.

Rnd 1: Ch 4, 23 dc in center of ring, join with 1 ss.

Rnd 2: Ch 4, 1 tr in next st, *skip 1 st, ch 2, 2 tr, rep from * 6 times, ch 2, join with 1 ss to top of turning ch.

Rnd 3: Ch 4, 1 tr in same place as turning ch, 2 tr in next st, *ch 3, (2 tr in next st) twice, rep from * 6 times, ch 3, join with 1 ss to top of turning ch.

Rnd 4: Ch 4, 1 tr in same place as the turning ch, 3 tr, *ch 3, 2 tr in next st, 3 tr, rep from * 6 times, ch 3, join with 1 ss to top of turning ch.

Rnd 5: Ch 4, 1 tr in same place as turning ch, 3 tr, 2 tr in next st, *ch 4, 2 tr in next st, 3 tr, 2 tr in next st, rep from * 6 times, ch 4, join with 1 ss to top of turning ch.

Rnd 6: Ch 4, (3 tr, ch 3, 1 tr) in same place as last tr, 3 tr, *ch 5, 4 tr, ch 3, 1 tr in the same place as the last tr, 3 tr, rep from * 6 times, ch 5, join with 1 ss to top of turning ch.

Rnd 7: Ss to next ch-3 sp [in block not ladder space], ch 7, (1 tr, ch 2) 6 times, 1 tr, ch 1, 1 sc in ch-5 sp, *ch 1, (1 tr, ch 2 in ch-3 sp) 7 times, 1 tr, ch 1, 1 sc in ch-5 sp, rep from * 6 times, join with 1 ss in fifth ch of ch 7.

Rnd 8: Ch 4, 1 sc in same sp, (1 sc, ch 2, 1 sc in next ch-2 sp) 6 times, (1 sc in ch-1 sp) twice, *(1 sc, ch 2, 1 sc in next ch-2 sp) 7 times, (1 sc in ch-1 sp) twice, rep from * 6 times, fasten off.

Old English Wheel ***

This is a very traditional English design.

Ch 10, join into a ring with 1 ss.

Stage 1: *Ch 20, 1 sc in center of ring, rep from * 11 times.

Stage 2: 15 dc in first loop, *ch 8, sc back in 6th st to form a picot, rep from * once, ch 19, turn work, fasten in fourteenth st [from hook], turn, 28 dc under ch loop, fasten with sc in first dc, ch 12, join in eighth st, *ch 5, sc under loop of ch 8, rep from * twice, turn; 1 sc, 9 dc, and 1 sc under each ch-5 sp, 1 sc in first st after cloverleaf, ch 6, sc in third ch of ch 5, *ch 8, sc in sixth st from hook, rep from * once, ch 2, and 15 dc under same ch of 20. All other points the same, except the 28 dc, which in second and succeeding points should be 14 dc, fasten with ss in fourth st of ch 6, 14 dc in same loop, fasten in first dc with ss, break thread after last point.

Stage 3: Dc on seventh and eighth of 14 dc of last row, ch 4, sc in fifth st of cloverleaf, *ch 8, sc in fifth st of next scallop of leaf, rep from * once, ch 4, rep from beg of row.

Stage 4: Dc on second dc of previous row, ch 2, dc on first sc, *ch 2, skip 1 st, dc on next st, repeat from * 8 times, ch 2, rep from the beg.

Stage 5: Sc on dc of previous row, ch 5, skip 2 ch, sc under next ch-2 sp, *ch 5, sc under next ch-2 sp, rep from * 7 times, ch 5, skip 2 ch, and rep from the beg.

Pineapple Circle *

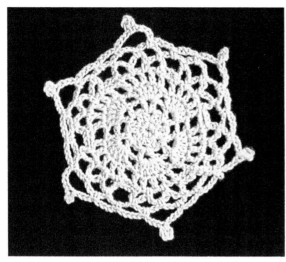

Old and new pattern books frequently feature a pineapple design, and no book on thread crochet would be complete without one. This is an extremely simple version. (Note that this is a design and not a stitch. If you come across something labeled a pineapple stitch it is probably referring to a cluster or a popcorn.)

Ch 5, join with 1 ss to form a ring.

Rnd 1: Ch 1, 5 sc in center of ring, join with ss to top of turning ch.

Rnd 2: Ch 4, 1 dc in same place, *(1 dc, ch 1, 1 dc) in next st, rep from * 4 times, join to third ch of ch 4 at beg of rnd with ss.

Rnd 3: Ss into ch-1 sp, ch 4, 1 dc in same sp, ch 2, *(1 dc, ch 1, 1 dc) in next ch sp, ch 2, rep from * 4 times, join to third ch of ch 4 at beg of rnd with ss.

Rnd 4: Ss in ch-1 sp, ch 3, 5 dc in the same space, ch 1, *6 dc in next ch-1 sp, ch 1, rep from * 4 times, join to beg of rnd with ss.

Rnd 5: Ch 4, (1 dc in next st, ch 1) 4 times, *ch 1, skip first dc of gr (1 dc in next st, ch 1) 5 times, rep from * 4 times, join to third ch of ch 4 at beg of rnd with ss.

Rnd 6: Ss to next ch-1 sp, *(ch 5, 1 sc in next ch-1 sp) 3 times, ch 3, skip next sp, 1 sc in next sp, rep from * 4 times, (ch 5, 1 sc in next ch-1 sp) 3 times, ch 3, join to beg of rnd with ss.

Rnd 7: Ss to next ch-5 sp, * (ch 5, 1 sc in next ch-5 sp) twice, ch 4, skip next sp, 1 sc in next sp, rep from * 4 times, (ch 5, 1 sc in next ch-5 sp) twice, ch 4, join to beg of rnd with ss.

Rnd 8: Ss to next ch-5 sp, *ch 8, ss in 4th ch of ch 8 just made, ch 4, 1 sc in next ch-5 sp, (ch 5, 1 sc in next sp) twice, rep from * 5 times, joining last ch 5 to beg of rnd with 1 ss. Fasten off.

Fan Square ***

This interesting motif begins as a circle. Then as you go along it changes to an octagon, with finally four fans added at the corners to make a square shape.

Ch 10, join into a ring with ss.

Rnd 1: Ch 4, (1 dc, ch 1 into center of ring) 15 times, join to third ch of ch 4 with ss.

Rnd 2: Ss into sp, ch 5, (1 dc, ch 2 in next ch sp) 15 times, join to third ch of ch 5 with ss.

Rnd 3: Ch 3, (2 dc in ch-2 sp, 1 dc on dc) 15 times, 2 dc in ch-2 sp, join to top of turning ch with ss.

Rnd 4: Ch 3, 1 dc in same place as starting chain, *ch 11, skip 5 dc, 2 dc cl in next st, rep from * 6 times, ch 11, join to top of turning ch with 1 ss.

Rnd 5: Ch 1, *15 sc in ch-11 sp, 7 sc in next ch-11 sp, ch 9, 1 ss into eighth sc of last 15 sc worked, [going backward], ch 3, (13 dc, 1 sc) in ch-9 sp just worked [to return to point in ch-11 sp from which ch 9 came]. 8 sc [to complete 15 sc required in ch-11 sp], rep from * 3 times, join rnd with ss.

Rnd 6: Ch 3, 1 dc in same place, *ch 5, (1 tr, ch 1 in next dc) 13 times, 1 tr in last st of fan, ch 5, 2 dc cl on top of cl in rnd 4, rep from * 3 times omitting last 2 dc cl, join to beg of rnd with ss.

Rnd 7: Ss into sp, ch 1, 6 sc in ch sp, *(1 picot, 1 sc in next ch-1 sp) 13 times, (7 sc in next ch-5 sp) twice, rep from * twice, (1 picot, 1 sc in next ch-1 sp) 13 times, 7 sc in next ch-5 sp, join to beg of rnd with ss.

Sunflower Lace **

Ch 6, join into a ring with 1 ss.

Rnd 1: Ch 5, 1 dc in ring, *ch 2, 1 dc in ring, rep from * 6 times, ch 2, 1 ss in third ch of ch 5.

Rnd 2: Ch 4, 3 tr in same space, *ch 2, 4 tr in next space, rep from * 6 times, ch 2, ss to top of turning ch.

Rnd 3: *Ch 5, 4 tr cl over tr of last rnd, ch 5, 1 sc in ch-2 sp, ch 5, rep from * 7 times, ss to last ch of ch 5 at beg of rnd.

Rnd 4: Ss to ch-5 sp, *ch 7, 1 sc in ch-5 sp to right of cluster, ch 5, 1 sc in ch-5 sp to left of cl, rep from * 7 times, 1 ss on ss to join.

Rnd 5: 2 ss in next ch sp, ch 3, 1 dc in same sp, ch 4, 1 sc on dc, (ch 4, 1 sc on last sc) twice, 2 dc in same ch sp, ch 2, *2 dc in next ch sp, ch 4, 1 sc on dc, (ch 4, 1 sc on last sc) twice, 2 dc in same ch sp, ch 2, rep from * 14 times, ss in top of turning ch at beg rnd.

Projects

The projects in this chapter—a stylish circular table center and three simple framed flower motifs—make ideal projects for beginners. You can use the same thread and hook for all three of the framed flower designs.

Circular Table Center

This circular table mat has an interesting textured center. The rest of it is fairly flat, making it ideal for use as a table center.

Materials:

• 1 x 75 g ball (approx. 338 yds.) No. 10 crochet cotton

• 1.75 mm (size 6) crochet hook

Gauge: Center of circle from rnds 1–9 inclusive = 12 cm (4¾")

Size: After pressing is 48 cm (19")

Ch 10, join with 1 ss to form ring.

Rnd 1: Ch 3, 2 dc in ring, *ch 1, 3 dc in ring, rep from * 4 times, ch 1, join with ss to top of ch 3 at beg of rnd, turn, ss into ch-1 sp just made, turn.

Rnd 2: Ch 3, 2 dc in same place, *ch 3, 3 dc in next ch sp, rep from * 4 times, ch 3, join with ss to top of ch 3.

Rnd 3: Ch 3, 1 dc in same place, 2 dc over dc, *2 popcorns in ch-3 sp, 2 dc in first of 3 dc, 2 dc, rep from * 4 times, 2 popcorns in ch-3 sp, join with ss to top of ch 3.

Rnd 4: Ch 3 to count as first dc in popcorn, complete popcorn, 2 dc, 1 popcorn in last dc, *ch 6, 1 popcorn, 2 dc, 1 popcorn, rep from * 4 times, ch 6, join to beg of rnd with ss.

Rnd 5: Ch 3 to count as first dc in popcorn, complete popcorn, 1 dc, 1 popcorn in last dc, *ch 4, 1 hdc in ch sp, ch 4, 1 popcorn, 1 dc, 1 popcorn in last dc, rep from * 4 times, ch 4, 1 hdc in ch sp, ch 4, join to beg of rnd with ss.

Rnd 6: Ch 3 to count as first dc in popcorn, complete popcorn, 1 popcorn in same place, *ch 3, (1 dc, ch 3) 3 times in hdc, 2 popcorns in dc, rep from * 4 times, ch 3, (1 dc, ch 3) 3 times in hdc, join rnd with ss.

Rnd 7: Ch 3 to count as first dc in popcorn, *ch 5, (1 dc on dc, ch 5) 3 times, 1 popcorn in center of 2 popcorns, rep from * 4 times, ch 5, (1 dc on dc, ch 5) 3 times, join rnd with ss.

Rnd 8: Ch 7, 1 dc in same place, *ch 5, (1 dc on dc, ch 5) 3 times, (1 dc, ch 5, 1 dc) in popcorn, rep from * 4 times, ch 5, (1 dc on dc, ch 5) 3 times, join rnd with ss.

Rnd 9: Ss into sp, ch 3, 8 dc in same space, *1 sc in next ch sp, 7 dc in next ch sp, 1 sc on dc, 7 dc in next ch sp, 1 sc in next ch sp, 9 dc in next ch sp, rep from * 5 times omitting last 9 dc, join rnd with ss.

Rnd 10: *Ch 5, 1 sc in central dc of group, ch 5, 1 sc in sc, rep from * to last group, ch 5, 1 sc in central dc of group, ch 3, 1 dc in ss joining last rnd (36 loops).

Rnd 11: *Ch 7, 1 sc in sp, rep from * to last sp, ch 4, 1 tr in ss at join.

Rep rnd 11 four times.

Rnd 16: 4 tr in sp, *1 sc in next sp, 5 tr in next sp, ch 5, 1 tr in sc, ch 5, 5 tr in next sp, rep from * 10 times, 1 sc in next sp, 5 tr in next sp, ch 5, 1 tr in sc, ch 5, join with ss to top of first tr.

Rnd 17: *(1 dtr, 2 tr, ch 2, 2 tr, 1 dtr) in sc, (ch 5, ss in next sp) twice, ch 5, rep from * 11 times, ch 3, 1 dc in tr at beg of rnd.

Rnd 18: *Ch 5, (3 tr, ch 2, 3 tr,) in ch-2 sp, (ch 5, 1 ss in next sp) 3 times, rep from * 11 times.

Rnd 19: *Ch 5, (3 tr, ch 2, 3 tr) in ch-2 sp, (ch 5, 1 ss in next sp) 4 times, rep from * 11 times.

Rnd 20: *Ch 5, (2 dc, ch 2, 2 dc,) in ch-2 sp, (ch 5, 1 ss in next sp) 5 times, rep from * 11 times. Mark this point and note the work should look as though it has begun to frill.

Rnd 21: *Ch 5, ss in ch-2 sp (ch 5, 1 ss in next sp) 6 times, rep from * 11 times.

Rnd 22: *Ch 5, ss in next sp, rep from * to end.

Rep rnd 22 another 10 times.

Rnd 33: Make sure you are in the ch sp that is directly above the first dc group in rnd 20. *(4 tr, ch 2, 4 tr) in next sp, (ch 5, ss in next sp) 5 times, ch 5, rep from * 11 times.

Rnd 34: *(3 tr, ch 2, 3 tr) in next sp, (ch 5, ss in next sp) 6 times, ch 5, rep from * 11 times.

Rnd 35: *(2 dc, ch 2, 2 dc) in next sp, (ch 5, ss in next sp) 7 times, ch 5, rep from * 11 times.

Rnd 36: *Ch 7, ss in next sp, rep from * to end.

Rep rnd 36 another 4 times.

Rnd 41: 2 sc in same space, 4 sc in each ch-7 sp to end, 2 sc in sp containing 2 sc, join with ss.

Rnd 42: Ch 3 to count as first dc, 4 dc, complete popcorn, *ch 4, 1 ss in sc, 5 dc in center of 4 sc, 1 ss in sc, ch 4, 1 popcorn in center of 4 sc, rep from * to last 4 sc gr of rnd, ch 4, 1 ss in sc, 5 dc in center of 4 sc, 1 ss in sc, ch 4, join to top of first popcorn with ss. Fasten off.

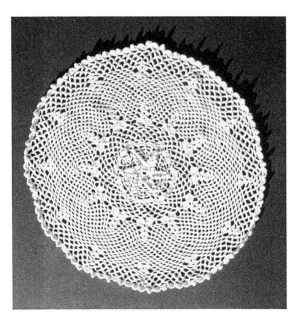

The finished table center.

Close-up of the central star design.

Framed Flower Motifs

Flower motifs are an ideal way to make a variety of creative items such as framed pictures and greeting cards, or they can be grouped together to form embellishments on fashion and household articles.

Materials:

• Small amounts of No. 10 crochet cotton in ecru

• 1.75 mm (size 6) crochet hook

• 3 picture frames, approximately 12 cm x 17 cm (4¾" x 6¾")

• ½ m (½ yd.) dark linen or hessian

Daisies

Start with the center. Ch 2.

Rnd 1: With RS facing, 6 sc in second ch from hook, ss to join [6 sc].

Rnd 2: Ch 1, 1 sc in same place, *2 sc in next sc, rep from * to end, ss to join [12 sc].

Rnd 3: Ch 1, *2 sc in next sc, 1 sc, rep from * 4 times, 2 sc in next sc, ss to join [18 sc].

Fasten off, leaving a long end for sewing.

To make petals, hold center with RS facing. Join in any sc.

Rnd 1: *Ch 8, sc in second ch from hook, 1 hdc, 1 dc, 2 tr, 1 dc, 1 hdc, skip next sc on center, ss in next st, rep from * 8 times, ss to first ch of ch 8 [9 petals].

Finish off, leaving a long end for sewing.

To make leaf, ch 18.

Row 1: 1 sc in second ch from hook, 2 sc, 3 dc, 5 tr, 3 dc, 3 sc.

Row 2: (Pointed edge around leaf) Continue working along other side of foundation ch, 2 sc, *(1 sc, ch 2, 1 sc) in next ch, continue to end of ch, around tip of leaf, and along each st to end, ss into first of the foundation ch.

To complete: Sew with cotton thread around circumference of center circle and draw up slightly to create a dome effect.

Violets

For the flower, use 1.75 mm crochet hook. Ch 5, join with ss into a ring. *Into ring work ch 4, 3 tr, ch 4, 1 sc, rep from * 4 times [5 petals worked].

The buds are worked in the same way as the flower, but when you finish, gather the outer edge of the ring into a little bud case prior to attaching it to the stem.

Ch 5, join into ring with ss.

Rnd 1: Ch 1, 7 sc in the ring, join with ss.

Rnd 2: *Ch 4, 1 sc in second ch from hook, 2 sc, 2 sc in last ch, 1 sc in sc of rnd 1, rep from * twice [3 points made].

To make leaves: For a small leaf, work to end of rnd 2. For a large leaf, continue to end.

Ch 8, 1 sc in second ch from hook, 6 sc.

Rnd 1: Using foundation ch again, place 1 sc and 3 dc in next st, 5 dc, 2 dc in the next ch, 2 dc in last ch (top of leaf), 2 dc in next sc, 2 dc, 2 dc in next st, 4 dc, ch 3, 1 sc, join with ss.

Rnd 2: Ch 1, 3 sc, 3 dc in next st, (2 dc in next st) 3 times, 5 dc, (2 dc in next st) 4 times, 6 dc, 2 dc in next st, 4 dc in next st, 1 sc in each of ch 3, 1 sc to end, join with ss. [For a small leaf, stop here.]

Rnd 3: Ch 1, 2 sc, 2 dc in next st, (3 dc in next st) 3 times, 2 dc in next st, 3 sc, 2 dc, 3 dc in next st, 2 dc, 3 sc, 1 dc, (2 dc in next st) 3 times, 2 sc, 2 dc, 3 dc in next st, 3 sc, 3 dc, 2 dc in next st, 3 dc in next st, 2 dc in next st, 4 sc, ss to join. Fasten off.

Iris

Starting at base of petal, ch 5, 1 sc in second ch from hook, sc to end.

Rnd 1: Ch 1, 1 sc in same place as joining ch, 3 sc in ch already used, (2 hdc, 2 dc, 2 hdc) in space created by remaining sc, 4 sc to end, join with ss. Fasten off.

For bud, ch 4, ss to form a ring.

Rnd 1: (RS) *Ch 5, 1 sc in second ch from hook, 3 sc, ss into ring, rep from * twice [3 spikes made]. Do not turn.

Work around first spike using ch 5 again. *4 sc, 2 hdc, 1 dc, 2 hdc in space made by last st, 4 sc, ss into ring, rep from * for 2 remaining spikes. Fasten off. Catch spikes together at top with thread.

To make leaf, ch 29, 1 sc in second ch from hook, 2 sc, 3 hdc, 3 dc, 11 tr, 3 dc, 2 hdc, sc to end.

To complete: Sew in ends. Place center spikes in center of lower petals.

To mount: Arrange flowers with their leaves and buds into an interesting spray on backing and secure with craft glue or sewing thread.

The finished, framed flower motifs. Top: iris, left: violet, right: daisy.

Chapter Four
Joining Motifs

Joining Motifs

When crochet was still a new medium, those venturing into it wanted to keep the look of the lace they were copying. This frequently meant that medallions would be connected in rows and the space left in the center of four circular motifs would have a small design incorporated later as a filler.

When connecting motifs in rows, the last round of a motif was worked so that some part of it could be divided to link into the previous motif. This avoided what might have been an obvious, ugly join and it reduced the number of ends that needed to be hidden inside the stitches. (Remember when working with thread that it is more difficult to hide the ends than when working the same item in yarn.)

Modern Methods

There are a variety of ways to connect motifs, but whichever you choose, make sure it joins the motifs as discreetly as possible. Select a method suitable for the shape of the motif and the finished article, bearing in mind what the finished item will be. For instance, if you are making a doily to go under a plant on an occasional table, it would be silly to connect the motifs in such a way that the most attractive part of the design is under the plant.

As with all good design, first select a suitable yarn for the purpose. For example, if vests or jackets are made with fibers that break easily, then it is possible that the garment may catch on a door handle and tear; this would not only disappoint the wearer but destroy hours of work. Next, select a motif that will fit the visual idea and its use. Finally, choose the joining method that you think is best for the motifs. For example, circular motifs frequently require an additional filler, depending on how you intend to place the circles against each other, while squares rarely require them but occasionally need half squares or triangles to make the edges either decorative or straight.

Joining Options

Sewing motifs together should be the last resort simply because of the nature of crochet stitches. Crochet stitches have their own elasticity and move in a way only crochet can, which is definitely not in the same way as knitted or woven fabrics, so when you sew crocheted motifs together you end up with stitches in a rigid and unnatural state. During wear or use, any movement that the crochet may wish to make becomes impossible because of the static nature of the sewn stitches. There are ways to make sewing stitches less immobile, but often these are unsuitable for joining crochet motifs together anyway.

Squares or Octagons with a Solid Edge

Crab stitch: One of the most interesting ways to connect squares or octagons is to crab stitch them together on the right side of the work, particularly if the last round of either of these two shapes is the same color on every motif. With squares, crab stitch just one side of the square to another square until there are enough connected squares to form the longest length required, and then join these strips together in the same way. The same process can be worked with octagons except that there are no long strips to join at the end because octagons leave a diamond-shaped space between them.

Single crochet: If you wish to avoid a frame, an alternative method is to single crochet the motifs together on the wrong side in the same way as when using the crab stitch.

Slip stitch: When the last row of the motif is a different color to its neighbor, working with a neutral color and placing slip stitches on the right side can produce an embroidered look. To obtain this finish, insert the hook under the single strand of yarn at the back of the stitch on the motif closest to you, and then insert the hook in the back loop of the connecting motif and work a slip stitch. (The back loop of the connecting motif is actually the strand nearest to you.) This allows the other strand to form a border or channel in which the slip stitch lies. Do watch the tension on this slip stitch. Slip stitches can be pulled too tight, gathering and puckering the motifs. If they are worked too loosely, they look untidy. Despite difficulties with tension, this is a good join and often worth persevering with.

Oversewing: Oversew each stitch together on the wrong side with a neutral thread, making sure the stitches are invisible on the right side of the work.

Joining Lacy Motifs

Crocheted connection: Work the complete first motif. Look at the last round worked and choose any chain spaces that will connect to another motif. Depending on the size and shape of the motif, it may be necessary to have one or two links. Unless it is a larger triangle, square, or rectangle, it is unusual to connect two motifs to form a line or strip with more than one or two connections. Divide the chain space evenly, taking the central chain for the slip stitch join. For instance, in a ch-3 sp, ch 1, 1 ss to join, ch 1, while for a ch-7 sp the division would be ch 3, 1 ss to join, ch 3.

Joining points: Occasionally the point of a lacy star might be a cluster or some other combination of stitches to form a solid, rather than a lacy, connection. It is immaterial whether these stitches form a textured or a flat area. Find the central stitch of the area to be connected to the next motif and work it until there are two loops on the hook (unless working a cluster when there will be more).

Insert the hook into the central stitch on the motif that is to be joined to the one being worked and pull the thread through all the loops on the hook. This completes the stitch on the motif being worked and firmly connects the other motif.

Note that all the stitches except the half double crochet can be worked to a point where there are only two loops left on the hook. If the connecting stitch is a half double crochet, leave the three loops on the hook and then insert the hook under the next stitch. When inserting the hook into the top of the central stitch on the motif you are connecting, insert the hook under two strands as normal unless the pattern indicates otherwise. When joining a cluster to a cluster, there will be more than two loops as you insert the hook into the opposite motif.

Joining Circles and Hexagons without a Filler

This method makes an effective shawl or triangular throw. You can choose whether to start at the point, joining two motifs to the first motif to make a miniature triangle and working upward to the final row of motifs, or whether to be brave and start with the longest row and work downward to the point. I like to work from the point upward so that if I think the item looks good without having to work another long row of motifs, I can stop. Working from the longest row to the point gives you no option but to continue until it is complete. The shapes will be connected once to the motif forming a row and once to each of the touching motifs, making three connections for each of the shapes.

Joining Hexagons without a Filler

Ideally, join hexagons at the points rather than in the center of an edge. This retains the shape of the motif better and still allows for the interesting diamond space between the motifs. On the last row you have a choice of keeping the edge undulating to follow the completed hexagon motifs or working half hexagons to make a straight edge.

Connecting Circles with a Filler

Circular motifs placed in columns and rows usually require a filler. The simplest filler is a ring of six chains with a number of single crochet stitches worked into it. The number of single crochets placed in the ring should be divisible by the number of joins you need to make. From each single crochet, make enough chains to reach to the motif when slightly stretched, join with a slip stitch, and make the same number of chains to return to the ring. Join with a slip stitch and repeat until all the link chains have been worked. The number of link chains will depend upon the size of the space left between the rows and columns of motifs.

Filler Stitches for Circles

Here are some filler stitches you may like to try for joining circles. The filler stitches are ideal for making winter scenes in the form of snowflakes; they are spidery and would need stiffening, but they look delightful hanging on a tree or in a window.

Simple Chain Link

Ch 4, join into a ring with ss.

Rnd 1: (Ch 21, ss into ring) 5 times, ch 10, (yo) 8 times, hook under ring, draw loop through, work off 2 loops at a time as in a dc.

Rnd 2: *Ch 13, ss into center ch of next loop, (ch 3, ss into same place) 3 times, rep from * 5 times, join with ss. This is the rnd used to connect the motifs. Split the central ch 3 of the clover into ch 1, 1 ss into motif, ch 1, and continue with rnd 2.

Filler for a More Angled Space

Ch 6, join into a ring with ss.

Rnd 1: *Ch 21, ss into a ring, ch 8, 1 ss into fourth ch from hook, (ch 4, 1 ss in last ss) twice, ch 4, 1 ss into ring, rep from * 3 times, fasten off. This is the round used to connect the motifs. It is the ch 21 that can be split into ch 10, 1 ss into motif, ch 10, and continue with rnd 1.

Twinkling Star Filler

Ch 4, join into a ring with ss.

Rnd 1: Ch 6, (1 dc into ring, ch 3) 5 times, join with ss into third ch of ch 6 at beg.

Rnd 2: (Ch 9, ss into fourth ch from hook, ch 5, ss into same place, ch 4, ss into same place, ch 5, ss into base of ch 9, ch 6, ss into ch-3 sp, ch 6, ss into next dc) 6 times, join with ss. This is the round used to connect the motifs. It is the ch 5 in the center of the trefoil point that can be split into ch 2, 1 ss into motif, ch 2, and continue with rnd 2.

Lacy Filler

Ch 4, join into a ring with ss.

Rnd 1: Ch 8 for first sc and ch-7 loop, (1 sc into ring, ch 7) 4 times, 1 sc into ring, ch 3, 1 tr into first ch of ch 8 at the beg of rnd.

Rnd 2: Ch 8 for first sc and ch-7 loop, (1 sc into the center ch of next loop, ch 7) 5 times, ss into second ch of first loop.

Rnd 3: *Ch 9, skip 3 ch, 1 ss into next ch, ch 7, ss into third ch from hook, (ch 3, ss into same place) twice, ch 4, 1 ss into second ch of next loop, rep from * 5 times. This is the rnd used to connect the motifs. It is the first of the ch 3 in the parentheses that can be split into ch 1, 1 ss into motif, ch 1, and continue with rnd 2.

Spidery Octagon

Cluster Array

Ch 4, join into a ring with 1 ss.

Rnd 1: Ch 5, 1 dtr in ring, *ch 4, 1 sc in ring, ch 4, 1 dtr in ring, rep from * twice, ch 4, join with 1 ss to second ch of ch 5 at beg of rnd.

Rnd 2: Ch 11, *1 sc in dtr, ch 7, 1 tr in sc, ch 7, rep from * twice, 1 sc in dtr, ch 7, join to fourth ch of ch 11. This is the round used to connect the motifs. It is the ch 7 that can be split into ch 3, 1 ss into motif, ch 3, and continue with rnd 2.

Ch 8, join into a ring with 1 ss.

Rnd 1: Ch 4, *1 dc into ring, ch 1, rep from * 14 times, join to third ch of ch 4 with ss.

Rnd 2: Ch 3, (1 dc, ch 3, 2 dc cl) all in same place as turning ch, skip 1 ch, 1 dc, ch 1, * ch 7, (2 dc cl, ch 3, 2 dc,cl) in next dc, rep from * 6 times, ch 7, join with ss to top of turning ch. This is the rnd used to connect the motifs. It is the ch 7 that can be split into ch 3, 1 ss into motif, ch 3, and continue with rnd 2.

Projects

A blanket and smart vest are the two projects in this chapter. They may look quite daunting at first because of their size, but they are actually quite simple to make. The blanket can easily be made into a larger blanket if desired.

Square Motif Crib Blanket

What parent could resist this blanket for a baby? Although this one is made in No. 10 thickness crochet cotton, it can easily be adapted to make a full-sized bedspread by using a thicker cotton and larger crochet hook. The motif has no tempting holes for little fingers to poke through, but the design still gives the impression of lace.

Materials:

• 2 x 50 g balls (approx. 450 yds.) of No. 10 cotton in white

• 1 x 50 g ball of No. 10 cotton in a contrasting color

• 24 small fabric rosebuds

• 1.75 mm (size 6) crochet hook

Size: 42 x 62 cm (16½" x 24½")

Gauge: One square measures 10 x 10 cm (4" x 4")

With white (A), ch 4, join into a ring with a ss.

Rnd 1: Ch 3, 2 dc into ring, *ch 1, 3 dc into ring, rep from * twice, ch 1, join with 1 ss to top ch of ch 3 at beg of row. Break off thread.

Rnd 2: Join contrast color (B) to any ch-1 sp, ch 3, (2 dc, ch 1, 3 dc) in same sp, ch 1, *(3 dc, ch 1, 3 dc) in next ch sp, ch 1, rep from * twice, join with 1 ss to top of turning ch. Break off thread.

Rnd 3: Join A to any corner ch-1 sp, ch 3, 1 dc, *ch 1, 4 dc in next ch-1 sp, ch 1, (2 dc, ch 1, 2 dc) in next ch sp, rep from * twice, ch 1, 4 dc in next ch-1 sp, (ch 1, 2 dc, ch 1) in next ch-1 sp [already occupied by 2 sts], join with ss to top of turning ch.

Rnd 4: Ch 3, 1 dc, *ch 1, 2 dc in next ch-1 sp, 4 dc, 2 dc in next ch-1 sp, ch 1, (2 dc, ch 1, 2 dc) in next ch sp, rep from * twice, ch 1, 2 dc in next ch-1 sp, 4 dc, 2 dc in next ch-1 sp, (ch 1, 2 dc, ch 1) in next ch-1 sp, join with ss to top of turning ch.

Rnd 5: Ch 3, 1 dc, *ch 1, 2 dc in next ch-1 sp, 8 dc, 2 dc in next ch-1 sp, ch 1, (2 dc, ch 1, 2 dc) in next ch sp, rep from * twice, ch 1, 2 dc in next ch-1 sp, 8 dc, 2 dc in next ch-1 sp, (ch 1, 2 dc, ch 1) in next ch-1 sp, join with ss to top of turning ch.

Rnds 6–9: Rep rnd 5, adding 4 dc to each side block of dc.

Work 23 more squares.

To join: Connect one side of a square to another with a row of ss, catching the back strand only of each stitch and being careful not to pull the ss too tight. Continue connecting squares to form a long strip of 6 squares. Once all the strips have been made, join the strips together in the same way to form a blanket of 4 x 6 squares.

Border

Rnd 1: Join B to any ss join. *Skip 3 sts, (3 dc, ch 1, 3 dc) in next st, skip 3 sts, 1 ss in next st, rep from * to corner, ch 1, (2 dc, ch 1, 2 dc) in corner st, 1 sc in next st, ** rep from * to ** 3 times, rep from * to start of rnd. [The last ss should be in same place as start of rnd.]

Rnd 2: Join A to any side ch-1 sp, *(3 dc, ch 1, 3 dc) in next ss, 1 sc in ch-1 sp, rep from * to end of rnd [As the corners are worked only with a sc, no increasing is necessary at corners of this rnd.]

Rnd 3: Ss to next ch-1 sp, *(3 dc, ch 1, 3 dc) in next sc, 1 sc in ch-1 sp, rep from *

to corner, ch 1, (2 dc, ch 1, 2 dc) in corner st, 1 sc in next ch sp,** rep from * to ** three times, rep from * to start of rnd.

Rnd 4: Work as rnd 2. Fasten off A.

Rnd 5: In B, crab stitch all around blanket. Fasten off.

To complete: Sew a small rosebud in the center of each square.

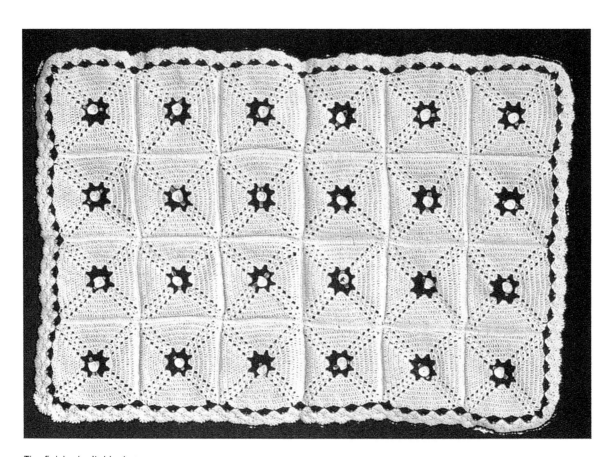

The finished crib blanket.

Flower Motif Vest

This vest design can be adapted to a longer length simply by adding more strips of 8 flowers to the base of the design, though if it becomes a full-length sleeveless coat, slits should be added into the pattern for ease of movement. These can be worked in the same way as the armholes.

Materials:

• 3 x 50 g balls (approx. 675 yds.) No. 10 cotton (makes 11–12 flowers with fillers)

• 1.75 mm hook

Bust size: One size to fit up to 96 cm (38"). A larger size can be made by working the same pattern with a 2.0 mm hook.

Length: Short (as illustrated): 40 cm (16"); medium: make an additional 16 flowers to form 2 more strips, which are added to the base of the vest to add another 22 cm (8") in length. For a longer length, make rows of 8 flowers for each 10 cm (4") you wish to add to the length.

Gauge: 1 flower motif measures 10 cm (4")

Special abbreviation: Sextruple trebles = sextr (wrap yarn around hook 6 times)

Motif 1: Ch 8, join into ring with 1 ss.

Rnd 1: Ch 12, (1 sextr, ch 3 into ring) 15 times, join to 9th ch of ch 12 with ss.

Rnd 2: Ss into sp, ch 3, 4 tr in same sp, (5 tr in next sp) 15 times, join to beg of rnd with ss.

Rnd 3: Ss to next st, ch 4, 3 dtr, (skip 1 st, ch 8, 4 dtr) 15 times, ch 8, join to beg of rnd with ss.

Rnd 4: Ss to center of 4 dtr group, (6 dc, ch 1, 6 dc) in ch-8 sp, 1 ss in center of 4 dtr group 16 times, join to beg of rnd with ss. Fasten off.

Motif 2: Work next circle to round 4. Join 2 consecutive petals of the ch of the motif being worked with 1 ss to 2 of the petals of previous motif.

Motifs 3–8: Work as second motif, ensuring you join petals lying exactly opposite the ones already joined in previous motif. The strip of 8 flowers will be for the 2 fronts and the back.

Motif 9: Work as second motif but join to 2 petals going up front. That is, skip 2 petals from the 2 already connected and join the next 2.

Motif 10: Work as second motif but join 2 petals to form a horizontal line from the ninth motif and 2 petals to form a vertical line from the flower on the strip of 8 flowers already joined.

Motifs 11–16: Work by attaching 4 of the 16 petals as described for the 10th motif.

Divide for armholes.

Motifs 17 and 18: Work as 9 and 10.

Motifs 19–22: Work as 9–12 (this leaves two flowers not connected for the armhole).

Motifs 23 and 24: Work as 9 and 10, leaving opening for next armhole.

Add 4 motifs for back to give 4 rows of flowers 4 flowers deep.

Fronts

Keeping connected petals in vertical and horizontal lines, attach 1 motif to armhole edge and connect the opposite 2 petals of this motif to the back armhole motif, to make the armhole. Connect another motif in a similar manner to complete the armhole and second front.

Filler

Ch 6, join into ring with 1 ss.

Rnd 1: Ch 1, 7 sc in center of ring, join with 1 ss.

Rnd 2: *Ch 8, 1 ss into any ch sp of a free petal, ch 8, 1 sc in next sc of ring, rep from * 7 times, fasten off.

Make a filler for any space where there are 8 petals free.

Half Filler for Edges

This connects the 4 loose petals encompassing the indentation at an edge.

Ch 6, join into ring with 1 ss.

Rnd 1: Ch 1, 7 sc in center of ring, join with ss.

Rnd 2: Starting to connect into right-hand side edge petal, ch 8, 1 ss into ch sp, ch 8, 1 sc in next sc of ring, (ch 6, 1 ss in ch sp of next free petal, 1 sc in next sc of ring) twice, ch 8, 1 ss into ch sp, ch 8, 1 sc in next sc of ring, 1 sc in each rem 4 sc in ring, fasten off.

Three-Quarter Filler for Armhole

This connects the central 6 loose petals at base of armhole split.

The finished vest.

Ch 6, join into ring with 1 ss.

Rnd 1: Ch 1, 7 sc in center of ring, join with 1 ss.

Rnd 2: Starting to connect into right-hand side edge petal, ch 8, 1 ss into ch sp, ch 8, 1 sc in next sc of ring, (ch 6, 1 ss in ch sp of next free petal, 1 sc in next sc of ring) 4 times, ch 8, 1 ss into ch sp, ch 8, 1 sc in next sc of ring, 1 sc in each rem 4 sc in ring, fasten off.

Fasten in all ends very securely.

Chapter Five
Irish Crochet

Irish Crochet

Irish crochet is based on the Venetian and guipure laces. That is, the motifs are made first and then connected by a background network of lace stitches, the most common of these being a chain and picot net. The subject is so large that it could fill a book by itself, so if you would like to learn more than I have space for, do take a look at the many old books that can be found in reference libraries, museums, and specialist textile collections. These will expand on the techniques and pattern designs included here. You may well find books covering traditional Irish crochet such as those written by Flora Klickmann and Eithne D'Arcy. Ask for the subject matter rather than a specific title, since this can often produce a treasure-trove of little-known books and writings. However, during the nineteenth and early twentieth centuries, most of the crochet patterns and know-how were contained in the pages of general needlecraft books.

When working from old patterns, always check what the designers mean by the various terms. For instance, in the later books produced by Mlle Riego, the term *double crochet* is introduced, but she uses it to mean inserting the hook under two threads without having first wrapped the yarn round the hook, producing a slip stitch. The term *raised crochet* has also changed meaning. As Mlle Riego uses the term, the double crochet stitches were worked over a cord, as on the final row of an Irish crochet motif. Since 1970, raised crochet means picking up the lower part of a whole stitch by inserting the hook from front to back around the stem part of the stitch to emerge at the front, thereby raising the stitch.

Here's a word of warning. If you wish to work Irish crochet in the traditional manner over padded cords, you will need to look for older designs because most of the patterns now available as Irish crochet are not worked over padded cords. Unless the design starts with padded cord for the center of the motifs and has a final row or round worked over a padded cord, it is not a traditional Irish crochet design but a quicker—and often just as lovely—adaptation. Working over a padded cord ensures that the motif can be cut away from the background, just as it is possible to cut away the motifs in a piece of Venetian or guipure lace. It has the further advantage of making it easier to connect the network when the background is being added to the motifs.

Some of the techniques of working Irish crochet changed around the time of the First World War. It was during this period that crocheters started omitting the padded cords. Also, it was found to be too time-consuming to place the individual motifs on a prepared shape of paper or cloth and then work the background net. Often the motifs were arranged in charming asymmetrical designs before the background was added. At this point, a chain and picot square were introduced to increase the speed of producing beautiful garments. This was achieved by making an Irish crochet rose, shamrock, or some other motif as a center for a square of chain and picots, sometimes with coronets added as markers for the four corners. The squares were then connected to form garments or household items such as bedcovers. Because of the way the background network of squares was connected, it was often quite difficult to recognize these designs as having been made by the quicker, more modern methods.

Almost 100 years later there are even more shortcuts to making beautiful designs based on Irish crochet but still called by that name. One of these came from the U.S., where the whole of the background was made first and the motifs sewn into place afterward.

Working Traditional Irish Crochet

It is still rewarding to work Irish crochet over padded cords. The following points should help make it more straightforward.

Padding: A number of motifs start with some form of padded center. The usual method suggested is to wrap the cotton several times around the end of a matchstick, and then insert the hook into the center of these threads to commence the actual crochet. However, if a tambour hook is used (a hook shaped like a stiletto), then it is possible to wrap the cotton around the thickest part of the hook, use your fingernails to keep the strands together, and slide these down to the tip of the crochet hook to start working the stitches into the ring immediately. This is not only quicker but it also means that you only need one tool rather than two. Occasionally you will need a larger diameter than the hook will allow, in which case you must use the method described for the grape design on page 87.

Thicker cottons: It is easier to use one thicker strand of cotton rather than several strands of the same thread as a padding cord—a mercerized thread of 5 or 8 thickness is easier to manage than 8 to 10 threads of 60.

Making a "knot": There are two methods of making a "knot" in Irish crochet. One is the bullion stitch and the other is a clones knot. In cotton, the latter seems to produce looser strands over the hook and therefore has a tendency to look untidy. If at all possible, use a bullion stitch in place of clones knots, which are not covered in this book. Sometimes, however, the design requires the shaggy look of clones knots, so make sure you substitute bullion stitches for the right reason.

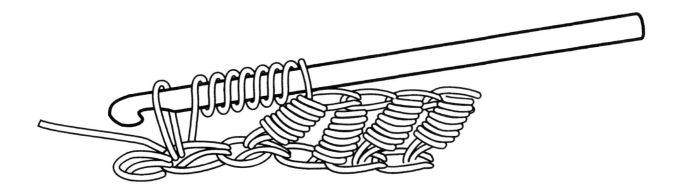

Bullion stitch.

The Irish rose: To make the traditional Irish rose, it is often more aesthetically pleasing if you insert the hook into the back of the stem of one of the crochet stitches to begin working chain loops, rather than going straight through a stitch. Then the hook insertion can't be seen at the front of the work.

Fashion items: When making a garment or fashion accessory such as a collar incorporating Irish crochet motifs or made solely of Irish crochet, you should make a toile first, to fit the body correctly. For a full garment it is usually best to make this in a softly draping fabric such as calico rather than from paper. It should be complete with any shaping, such as darts or tucks. Paper can be used for accessories, but it is not as easy to work with as fabric and may tear. Arrange the motifs on the toile in a pleasing design before adding the background network. I suggest you secure these motifs quite firmly to the fabric before starting the background. There is nothing more frustrating than to see a carefully arranged design drop to pieces the moment the background is being constructed. (For additional information on how to arrange the motifs to best advantage, see the detachable collar on page 90.)

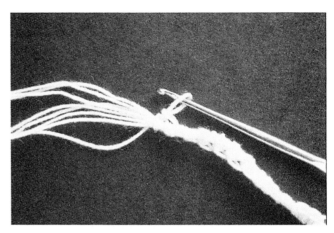

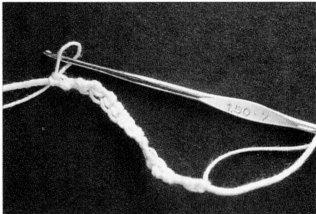

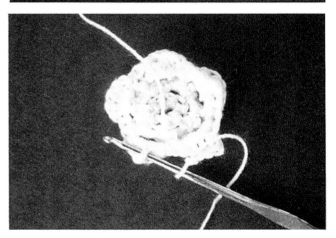

Top: Working over a padded cord (traditional method).
Middle: Working over padded cord (modern adaptation).
Bottom: Connecting the chain loop for the next round of petals.

Rose Patterns

The motif in Irish crochet that most people know is the Irish rose. Inevitably the rose has many variations and there is probably no one living today who could tell us precisely which of the rose patterns was the original rose that became such a hallmark of Irish crochet. Different regions had different variations of the rose pattern, but also people would not necessarily remember the verbal instructions and so the rose would look slightly different depending on who crocheted it. Roses can be small or large depending on how many layers of petals are worked.

Small Rose

Ch 8, join into a ring with 1 ss or work over a padding cord shaped into a ring. Into ring, work 12 sc.

Rnd 1: Ch 5, skip 1 sc, 1 sc in next stitch, work this all around, making 6 holes in total.

Rnd 2: 1 sc, 1 dc, 1 sc into every loop, join with ss.

Rnd 3: Ch 6, 1 sc on sc between petals, make ch come behind petal, rep all around.

Rnd 4: 1 sc, 1 hdc, 6 dc, 1 hdc, 1 sc in every loop, join as before. Fasten off.

Medium Rose

Ch 8, join into a ring with 1 ss or work over a padding cord shaped into a ring. Into ring, 12 sc.

Rnd 1: Ch 5, skip 1 sc, 1 sc in next stitch, work this all around, making 6 holes in total.

Rnd 2: 1 sc, 1 dc, 1 sc into every loop, join with 1 ss.

Rnd 3: Ch 6, 1 sc on sc between petals, make ch come behind petal, rep all around.

Rnd 4: 1 sc, 1 hdc, 6 dc, 1 hdc, 1 sc in every loop, join as before. Fasten off.

Rnd 5: Ch 8, 1 sc behind petal all around.

Rnd 6: 1 sc, 1 dc, 8 tr, 1 dc, 1 sc in every loop, join. Fasten off.

Large Rose

The rose is ideal for the center of a network square of chains and picots so I have provided details on making this type of network with this large rose pattern.

Ch 8, join into a ring with 1 ss or work over a padding cord shaped into a ring. Into this work 12 sc.

Rnd 1: Ch 5, skip 1 sc, 1 sc in next stitch, work this all around, making 6 holes in total.

Rnd 2: 1 sc, 1 dc, 1 sc into every loop, join with 1 ss.

Rnd 3: Ch 6, 1 sc on sc between the petals, make ch come behind petal, rep all around.

Rnd 4: 1 sc, 1 dc, 6 tr, 1 dc, 1 sc in every loop, join as before. Fasten off.

Rnd 5: Ch 8, 1 sc behind every petal all around.

Rnd 6: 1 sc, 1 dc, 8 tr, 1 dc, 1 sc in every loop, join.

Rnd 7: Ch 10, 1 sc behind every loop.

Rnd 8: 1 sc, 1 dc, 10 tr, 1 dc, 1 sc in every loop, join.

Rnd 9: Ch 11, 1 sc behind every petal, join.

Rnd 10: 1 sc, 1 dc, 12 tr, 1 dc, 1 sc in every loop.

Rnd 11: Ch 12, 1 sc behind every petal.

Rnd 12: 1 sc, 1 dc, 14 tr, 1 dc, 1 sc in every loop, join.

*Ss to fourth st of first petal on final layer, (ch 7, ss in fifth ch from hook to form p) twice, ch 2, 1 sc into fourth dc on opposite side of same petal, ch 7, ss in fifth ch from hook, rep from * all round until it is time to work last ch lp containing 2 p. (Ch 7, ss in

fifth ch from hook to form p) twice, 1 dc in ss at beg of the rnd. This completes large rose and forms first rnd of p background network.

Network Background

How many rounds you work depends on how large you want your square to be. First mark where the four corners will be placed.

Rnd 2 of network: Turn work and ss to center of loop just worked. Turn work, (ch 7, ss in fifth ch from hook to form p) twice, ch 2, 1 sc into center of next ch loop going into space between 2 p. If it is a corner loop, place an additional loop in same place. Experiment for yourself, since some people find it better to go to either side of the p for an extra corner loop, while others prefer an extra loop just in the center. This is purely a matter of personal choice.

Subsequent rnds: Repeat rnd 2 of network until square is size you require.

Irish rose motif in various sizes.

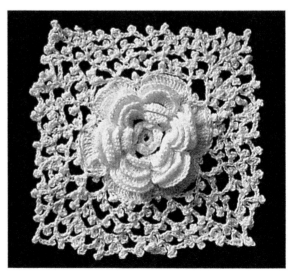

Irish rose in the center of a square of chain and picot network.

Grape Design

Individual padded circles are made to represent one grape in a bunch. The number of grapes depends on the size of the finished article.

Stage 1: To make each grape, you need the handle of a smooth, round pen or pencil. If you are fortunate enough to have one shaped like a stiletto, then that will be best. I have a small craft knife with a sheath that is ideal because the handle is smoothed and shaped in this way. The shaped handle allows you to produce grapes of different sizes because you can wrap the thread around the handle at different points to make them smaller or larger as desired.

Stage 2: Wrap thread around handle 13–15 times. Carefully nip these threads together between thumb and forefinger of hand holding thread. Without breaking off thread, insert crochet hook into hole and draw thread through, ch 1. Make as many sc as will fit into hole without spaces between them and without them buckling.

Stage 3: Make as many grapes as you need; then stitch the grapes into a bunch. If desired, you can attach a stem to make the motif look as though it has just come from the vine.

Shamrock

Try the following method for an effective shamrock motif that does not have any ends to darn in.

Stage 1: Make a slip knot, making sure it slips from the tail end of the thread and not the ball end. To do this, simply follow the instructions on making a slip knot on page 25 but this time wrap the tail end of the thread over the continuous thread running from the ball.

Stage 2: Ch 2. With the smooth side of ch facing, work into top strand of second ch from hook (the slip knot), 17 dc, 1 sc, and fasten off. If slip knot has been made correctly, the loop will get larger the more stitches you place in it. Draw string sufficiently tightly to make a well-shaped shamrock leaf.

Stage 3: Make a second shamrock leaf in exactly the same way.

Stage 4: Make third shamrock leaf but do not fasten off.

Stage 5: Link 3 leaves together by inserting hook through central hole (the starting and finishing point of the leaves) and join with ss. There should be 5 long strands running from this point plus the working thread. Over 5 strands of cotton, work as many sc as required for length of stem needed. Fasten off working thread and run this end up through the middle of stem to complete. Cut rest of threads level with last stitch worked.

Leaf

Row 1: Ch 16. 1 sc in second ch, 1 sc in each ch to end. Add 2 sc in ch of last sc, sc down other side, ch 1, turn.

Subsequent rows: Working in back loops only from this point on, 11 sc, leaving the last 3 sts unworked. Ch 1 turn, sc to other end, 3 sc in center end st, 11 sc down other side, leaving 3 sts unworked. *Ch 1, turn, sc to other end, 3 sc in center end st, sc down other side, leaving 3 sts unworked. Rep from * until leaf is fat enough for your design. The leaf in the picture has 8 rows, giving 3 points on each side plus the tip of the leaf.

Rosebud

Make a small padded ring using the thickest part of the hook to wrap the thread around. Work 15 sc, join with ss.

Rnd 1: 1 sc, 1 dc, 1 tr with ch 3 picot in the top, 1 tr, 1 dc (rep twice more, making 3 petals).

Working Pointers

Tension: Check that you have not made the chains in the network too tight. If your fingers hurt, then the chains are too tight.

Hook insertion: Remember to insert the hook into the chain space—the hook goes under the chains and not into them.

Counting rows: Should your background be in unbroken rows, for instance, if you have decided to sew the motifs onto a background rather than work the background afterward in the traditional way, then counting the rows is easier if you count the diamond-shaped holes and multiply by two.

Measuring: Drop the finished piece of crochet onto a smooth top. Assuming it has dropped flat, measure it where it lies without trying to smooth it out across the width or length. Do remember, however, that often this kind of crochet looks better stretched, so you would need to make the piece a little smaller than required for the best results, particularly for household items.

Projects

The following projects can't be written as stitch-by-stitch patterns. They can be worked either in the traditional way over a padded cord or in the newer way without the padded cords. They leave room for you to decide for yourself how to complete them, but they contain all the information you need to re-create the articles shown.

Napkin Rings

These napkin rings are the work of Margaret Hughes and are included here in posthumous recognition of her excellent work. The materials are sufficient to make at least four napkin rings. Choose any motif from any Irish crochet pattern. As you can see from the photograph, Margaret made a set of six. Although the motifs are different, making it easy to identify them, they are all made in the same way.

Materials:

• 1 x 25 g ball (approx. 113 yds.) of white 20 cotton

• 1 x 25 g ball (approx. 113 yds.) of 20 cotton in a contrasting color for the lining

• 1.25 mm (size 9 or 10) crochet hook

Size: To fit a standard napkin

Gauge: 9 sts to 2 cm (¾") and 5 rows to 1 cm (⅜") worked in sc

Lining

In contrast thread, ch 56. Carefully join into a ring with ss, making sure ch has not twisted. (NB: you can work the first row of sc before joining into a ring, joining the sc and using the end left from the slip knot to join the chain.) Work 20 rnds of sc. Fasten off.

Cover

Make the motif following the instructions in the original pattern. Finish the cover by making a background of chains and picots that fill the area so that the cover piece is the same size as the lining, working the last row of chain and picot so that they join to the start of the tube. (See "Joining Lacy Motifs" on page 73.)

Assembly

Slide the cover over the lining and work 1 rnd of sc to sandwich both pieces of crochet together on either side of the tube.

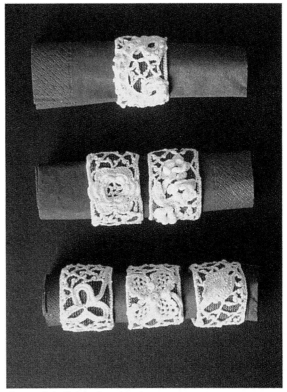

A set of six finished napkin rings.

Detachable Collar

This collar is ideal for embellishing a winter top. It gives you the chance to be creative because it is extremely difficult to reproduce an exact replica when working Irish crochet in this manner—the finished collar will be unique. The project is based on the motifs in this book with the Irish rose as the main feature. For a lighter weight collar and finer look, work in No. 20 cotton and a 1.25 mm crochet hook.

Materials:

• 1 x 75 g ball (approx. 338 yds.) of No. 10 cotton

• 1.75 mm (size 6) crochet hook

Stage 1: Make a toile out of paper or cloth that is the exact size and shape of the collar you wish to make.

Stage 2: Choose a selection of motifs to use on the collar from the stitch library, or use motif patterns from other books.

Stage 3: Arrange the motifs in such a way that the heaviest-looking motifs are placed at the points or curve of the collar, away from the neck edge. These motifs may or may not be the largest in size, but they should look the heaviest from a distance. Use these motifs as your starting point.

Stage 4: Arrange the remaining motifs around the edge of the collar to form a border or band of motifs that should be touching or almost touching each other.

Stage 5: If the collar is deep, you will need to include more motifs to balance the shape.

Stage 6: You may like to see how the design looks on a person at this point. Sometimes what looks attractive on a flat surface can look very different when it is shaped on an object (or person).

Stage 7: Having satisfied yourself that the motifs are balanced and will make an attractive collar, fill in the spaces with a chain and picot edge as described both for the large Irish rose with its background (pages 85–86) and also for the little scatter cushion in the next project.

Stage 8: Depending on how deep you have decided to make your collar, you can complete the neck edge either with a string of small roses or with a braid.

Stage 9: It is possible to work a simple row of single crochet into the chain loops, but this will require constant vigilance on your part if you are to have an even border. On the rare occasions that I use this method, I tend to complete the edge with a row of crab stitches because these can skip a stitch without it being obvious and thus help to correct any irregularities that may have occurred in the working of the single crochet row.

The completed collar.

Pillow

This pattern is adapted from a Flora Klickmann fern design. The cushion in the photograph has a blue velvet lining and backing but any richly colored fabric would work equally well.

Materials:

- 1 x 75 g ball (approx. 338 yds.) of 10 cotton (bedspread weight)

- 1.75 mm (size 6) hook

- 28 cm (11") pillow form

- 61 cm (24") contrast fabric in a single color

Size: Small 25 cm (10") pillow

Stage 1: Over a padding cord (pc), work 20 sc for stem, 35 sc, **3 sc to turn, 3 sc, *ch 1, 1 dc, 1 tr, (1 p of ch 3 on top of tr, 1 tr, 1 dc, ch 1, 1 sc*. Rep from * to * 6 times, turn.

Stage 2: 10 sc for stem **, 30 sc, rep from ** to ** 6 times only, 25 sc, rep from ** to ** 5 times only, 20 sc, rep from ** to * 4 times, 4 sc for stem. 20 sc, rep from ** to * 4 points. This is the center frond.

Stage 3: Continue by working over a pc into the stem of the corresponding fronds on the opposite side. Carefully work down the other side of the central stem by attaching cotton at the stem and making points to match the other side, always putting the hook over the cord and working in sc. Fasten off the cotton at the end of the frond.

Picot Filling

If your lining material is colorfast, you can attach the fern to it and work the background directly onto it, completing the pillow cover with another piece of fabric after all the crochet has been worked. Alternatively, you will need to have either a piece of paper or a piece of fabric that has been accurately marked out to the size required.

Sew the fern firmly onto your square foundation, arranging the fronds as shown in the picture on page 92. Work a background net of ch and p as a filling. The background here is made of (ch 7, 1 sc in fourth ch from hook) twice, ch 3, 1 sc at point of anchoring this loop. You may find it necessary to work 3 p instead of 2 for turning at the end of the rows.

Border

It is important to take care with the first rnd of this border. The tendency is to place too many sc over the pc, which results in the border frilling.

Rnd 1: Work sc over a pc, linking with ss to any appropriate ch and p loops from the background to make the border straight. Join with ss.

Rnd 2: Ch 4, *skip 2 sts, 1 dc, ch 2, rep from * to end, placing (1 dc, ch 2, 1 dc) in corner st. Join with ss to second ch of ch 4 at beg of rnd.

Rnd 3: Work 2 sc over a pc and ch of previous rnd (3 sc if necessary to keep edge straight). Join with ss and fasten off.

Irish Crochet

The finished pillow, with a blue velvet background.

Chapter Six
Crochet Imitating Other Types of Lace

Crochet Imitating Other Types of Lace

The crochet hook does not respect the ideas belonging to other crafts and it seems to revel in copying designs from them, in particular from the craft of lace making. Crochet even took the name of the lace in many instances. In fact, it is interesting to discover just how many types of lace crochet are actually copied, including tatting (worked with a shuttle) and netting (a form of knotting).

Needle-made laces: The group of laces known as needle-made lace are made in different ways and are often peculiar to a particular geographical region. Some of the more familiar names have been used to describe crochet patterns—reticella, filet, Mignardaise, and Venetian. Crochet also incorporated braids but used a machine-made version. The picot edgings made them ideal for use in copying some of the laces such as Mignardaise. (Mignardaise lace used handmade braids to form the base of its patterns.) Sadly these braids are no longer available, and therefore I cannot include designs incorporating them. Should you find some of the old braids in a secondhand store, you may like to experiment—the old Weldons patterns are a great source of inspiration.

Lace braid: Hairpin crochet lace is a method of copying a lace braid and producing extended loops instead of the shorter picots. This is a delightful way of working crochet but it has so many variations that it is not possible to include the subject here.

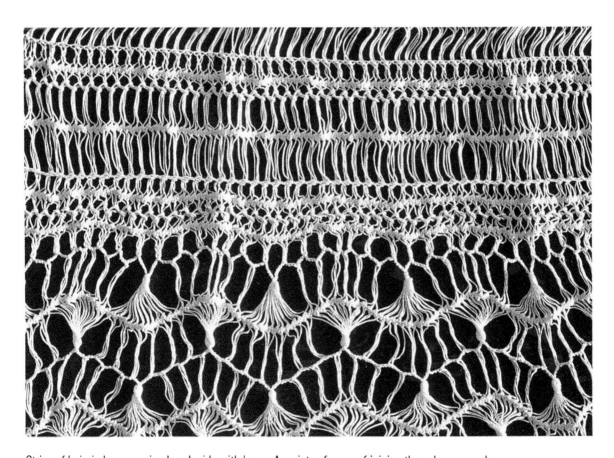

Strips of hairpin lace, copying lace braids with loops. A variety of ways of joining these loops are shown.

Tenerife lace was the inspiration for this bedspread (detail below) made using yarn and a daisy loom.

Tenerife lace: The daisy wheel or daisy loom was a means of making florets that could be crocheted together to copy Tenerife lace. The boldly colored bedspread shown left and below was made using yarn instead of the thread normally associated with Tenerife lace.

Needle laces: Some needle laces were applied to a net background. This idea was copied in crochet by making both the motifs and the netting together with a crochet hook and fine thread. Filet crochet is the perfect example of this (see pages 36–51).

Venetian and guipure lace: These were imitated in Irish crochet (see pages 82–92).

Solomon's knot: This is the pirate version of netting and is particularly useful for incorporating a very lacy design quickly and comparatively easily.

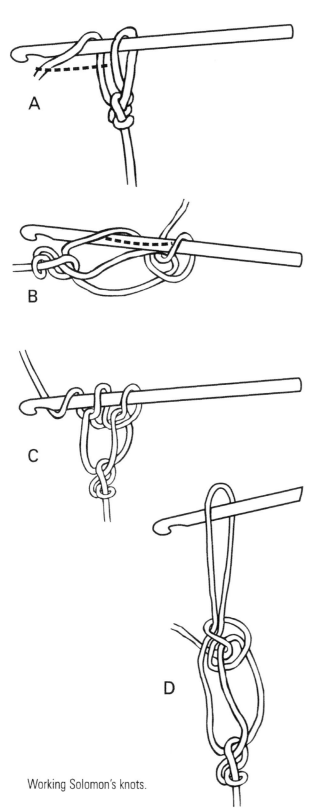

Working Solomon's knots.

Working Solomon's knot crochet

To make a Solomon's knot, work one chain and extend this to the length required—approximately 5 cm (2") long. As can be seen in diagrams A and B, the chain consists of a continuous loop and a single thread lying behind it. Insert the hook between the loop and the single thread, as shown. Yarn over hook, draw through to the front to have 2 loops on the hook (diagram C), yarn over hook, draw through 2 loops, bringing the work back to 1 loop and extend (diagram D).

The foundation row could be a chain, but on the whole it is better to use the knots themselves to keep the soft, lacy look throughout. The number of Solomon's knots for the foundation chain depends on the length of the article being made. These should be slightly longer than the chains being extended in the main body of the work; otherwise the base row will be tight. Make sure that all the extended chains you make are all the same length.

Anchoring sc to Form the Knot

Follow either option 1 or option 2.

Option 1: Add 2 more Solomon's knots for turning, work a single crochet into the center of the third knot down from the hook. Continue the foundation row by making two knots and anchoring into the last knot in the next foundation knot with a single crochet.

Option 2: Alternatively, work two more Solomon's knots as for the first method, but link the knots by working a single crochet in the chain before the knot and a further single crochet in the chain after the knot. This method makes the joining of the knots larger and more prominent than the first.

Whichever method you follow, you will need to work three Solomon's knots to turn in order to keep the sides straight. Continue in this manner, anchoring the next row into the pointed part containing a knot.

Crocheted "Tatting" Edging

I have chosen to put this edging in as an illustration of crocheted tatting, since it is identical in appearance to one of the basic edgings made by a beginner to tatting.

Base row: Make a ch that can be divided by 9, join into a ring with 1 ss. (This particular pattern is more difficult to work if you want it as a straight edge.)

Rnd 1: *Ch 3, skip 2 ch, 1 sc in next ch, rep from * to end, placing last sc at starting point of rnd. Alternatively this can be worked into fabric directly with 1 sc and ch 3 to make small ch-3 sp.

Rnd 2: Ch 20, *join with ss into third sc (to give 2 half rings and a loop), ch 5, join into sixth ch up on the previous ch to form a ring, ch 15, rep from * to end, finishing with ch 10, link to sixth ch of ch 20, ch 5, 1 ss in same place as starting point.

Rnd 3: Into the first ring make (4 sc, 1 p, 3 sc), *(4 sc, 1 p, 3 sc, 1 p twice, 4 sc) all in ch-10 sp, (3 sc, 1 p, 4 sc) in ring, letting stitches lie on left-hand side of the ring, 1 ss in base of ring and in rnd 1, (4 sc, 1 p, 3 sc) to complete ring. Rep from * to end.

Crocheted "tatting" edging.

Square "Honiton Lace" Design

Other than filet lace and Irish crochet motifs, the square motifs copied from the designs in Honiton lace are probably the next best known. (Honiton is a town in Devon, England, that is worth a visit if you are interested in these laces.)

Make a slip knot that does not slide from the tail end (see page 25).

Rnd 1: Ch 10, 1 tr in ninth ch from hook. (ch 5, 1 tr in same place as first tr) 3 times. ch 5, 1 ss in fifth ch of ch 10 at beg of rnd to form ring.

Points

Row 1: Ch 1, 8 sc, skip 1 st, turn.

Row 2: Ch 1, 7 sc, skip 1 st, turn.

Subsequent rows: Continue reducing the rows by 1 st until 1 st remains, fasten off.

Subsequent points: Work 3 more points over each space but do not break off at the last point.

Completion: *Ch 4, skip 1 row end, 1 sc in next row end, rep from * around both sides of all 4 points with 4 loops on each side of each point. Fasten off.

Corners

Join yarn to tip of any point, *ch 20, turn. Work back along ch. 1 tr in eighth ch from hook, ch 4, 1 tr in same place, ch 5, skip 3 sc in ch, 1 sc in next ch, turn. 6 sc in ch-5 sp, 3 sc in ch-4 sp, ch 3, 1 sc to connect loops in sc between points at base, ch 3, 3 sc in same ch-4 sp, 6 sc in last loop, ch 8, 1 sc in tip of next point, rep from * 3 times.

Next rnd: 10 sc in ch-8 sp, 8 sc in ch-4 sp, 3 sc in ch used twice on previous rnd for corner, 8 sc in next sp, 10 sc in ch-8 sp, rep from * 3 times.

Next rnd: Ch 5, * skip 2 sts, 1 dc in next st, ch 2, rep from * to corner, 1 dc, ch 2, 1 dc, ch 2, skip 2 sts**, rep from * to ** until rnd is complete. Join with ss.

Last rnd: Ch 1, 2 sc in next sp, *3 sc in each sp to corner, 5 sc in corner sp, rep from * to end of rnd. Note: you may find you require 1 sc less every third or fourth sp in order to keep work flat.

Alternative "Honiton" Design

Ch 5, join into a ring with 1 ss.

Rnd 1: Ch 4, 4 tr in ring, ch 4, *5 tr in ring, ch 4, rep from * twice, join to top of ch 4 with ss.

Rnd 2: Ch 4, 4 tr cl over 4 tr, *ch 7, 1 sc in ch-4 sp, ch 7, 5 tr cl over 5 tr, rep from * twice, ch 7, 1 sc in ch-4 sp, ch 7, join with ss.

Rnd 3: 1 ss into next sp, ch 1, 8 sc in space, *4 sc in next sp, turn back with ch 10, 1 ss in center sc of 9 sc gr, turn, and into this ch-10 sp work (1 sc, 1 hdc, 2 dc, 6 tr, 2 dc, 1 hdc, 1 sc), 5 sc, 9 sc in next ch sp, rep from * 3 times, omitting last 9 sc. Join with ss.

Rnd 4: Ch 10, *skip 2 sts, (1 tr, ch 1) 8 times, 1 tr, ch 5, 1 tr in sc over top of cluster, ch 5, rep from * to end, omitting last ch 5, 1 ss in center of ch 10 at beg of rnd.

Rnd 5: *8 sc in ch-5 sp, (ch 3, 1 sc in ch-1 sp) 8 times, 8 sc in ch-5 sp, rep from * 3 times, join with ss.

A selection of crochet motifs inspired by Honiton lace.

"Tenerife Lace" Coaster

To make a crochet version of a delicate wheel typical of Tenerife lace, you would need very fine cotton indeed and a 0.60 mm hook. Using a thicker thread and larger hook size, you can make a pleasing coaster.

Ch 24, join into a ring with 1 ss.

Rnd 1: Ch 3, 41 tr in the center of the ring, join with 1 ss.

Rnd 2: Ch 3, 1 dc in next st, *ch 3, skip 1 st, 2 dc, rep from *12 times, ch 3, join to top of turning ch with ss.

Rnd 3: Ch 3, 1 dc on dc, *ch 4, skip ch sp, 2 dc, rep from * 12 times, ch 4, join to beg of rnd with ss.

Rnd 4: Ch 3, 1 dc on dc, *ch 5, skip ch sp, 2 dc, rep from * 12 times, ch 5, join to beg of rnd with ss.

Rnd 5: Ch 3, 1 dc on dc, *ch 7, skip ch sp, 2 dc, rep from * 12 times, ch 7, join to beg of rnd with ss.

Rnd 6: Ch 3, 1 dc on dc, *ch 9, skip ch sp, 2 dc, rep from * 12 times, ch 9, join to beg of rnd with ss.

Rnd 7: Ch 7, 1 sc in dc, *9 sc in ch-9 sp, 1 sc, ch 7, 1 sc, rep from * 12 times, 9 sc in ch-9 sp, join with ss and fasten off.

"Tenerife lace" coaster.

Projects

The two projects in this chapter imitate two different styles of lace. The cuffs of the gloves feature a design used in Brussels lace and an embellishment from Irish crochet, which was itself a copy of some of the guipure and Venetian laces. The bedspread is made using a circle shape and design based on Tenerife lace. You can work the circles according to the instructions give for the coaster opposite, or you can use a daisy loom.

Brussels Lace Gloves

Many people look for lacy gloves in white for weddings and other religious ceremonies and formal events. Here is a design that is not difficult to do and is exactly right for those special occasions.

Materials:

- 1 x 25 g ball (approx. 143 yds.) mercerized cotton in No. 20 thickness

- 1.25 mm (size 9 or 10) crochet hook

- 0.5 m (½ yd.) fine round hat elastic or strong shirring elastic. For a larger hand, you may just break into a second ball of cotton, and would need a 1.50 mm hook

Size: To fit a size 6 hand. For a larger size (7), use a 1.50 mm hook.

Gauge: 7 sts and 11 rows to 2.5 cm (1") worked over ch lp pattern.

Left-Hand Thumb

Ch 4, join with 1 ss to form ring.

Rnd 1: Ch 3, (ch 1, 1 dc in ring) 7 times, ch 1, ss into top of ch 3.

Rnd 2: (Ch 3, 1 sc in next sp) 8 times.

Rnd 3: *Ch 5, 1 sc in next loop, rep from * to end.

Place a marker at beg of rnd 3, continue working rnd 3 another 12 times.

Rnd 16: Ch 5, 1 sc in same loop for inc, *ch 5, 1 sc in next loop, rep from * to end.

Rep rnd 16 twice. Fasten off.

First Finger

Work as for thumb but rep rnd 3 another 17 times, or until finger reaches required length. Fasten off.

Second Finger

Work as for thumb but rep rnd 3 another 18 times, or until finger is required length. Do not fasten off. Join to previous finger by placing the 2 edges together, and working (ch 1, 1 sc into next loop of both fingers, ch 1, 1 sc into same 2 loops of 2 fingers) twice. Fasten off.

Third Finger

Work as for the first finger and join to second finger.

Fourth Finger

Ch 4, ch 1, ss into top of ch 3.

Rnd 1: Ch 3, (ch 1, 1 dc in ring) 6 times.

Rnd 2: (Ch 3, 1 sc in next sp) 7 times.

Continue working ch 5 loops for 15 rounds or until required length. Join to third finger, but do not fasten off.

The Hand

Rnd 1: Work 24 ch-5 loops along bottom of fingers, finishing immediately below fourth finger. This is the point where a manufactured glove would have its seam. Place a marker here as all rnds now begin from this point.

Work rnd 1 another 11 times.

Rnd 13: Work 9 ch-5 loops, connect next ch-5 loop into a loop at base of thumb and also into next loop of hand, joining them together. Connect next 5 loops of hand and thumb by working (ch 1, 1 sc into hand and ch 1, 1 sc into thumb loop) twice into each of 4 loops. Leaving 5 loops of thumb unworked, finish rnd with ch 5-loops along remaining loops of hand.

Rnd 14: Work ch-5 loops in loops across back of hand, mark this point, work ch-5 loops along edge of thumb, mark this point, work ch-5 loops to end of rnd.

Rnd 15: Work ch-5 loops to marker, ch 5, dec by working next sc into both of next 2 loops together, work 6 ch-5 loops, dec as before at marker, finish rnd.

Work 2 rnds in loops.

Rnd 18: As 14th rnd, placing dec immediately over previous dec giving only 5 loops between dec.

Work 2 rnds without dec.

Rnd 21: As 14th rnd, but with 4 loops between the 2 decs.

Work 2 rnds without dec.

Rnd 24: Work in loops to dec, 1 dec, finish round in loops, ss into next loop.

Work 2 rnds without dec.

Rnd 27: Cut elastic in half. Make 2 halves into rings to form wristlets. Place each ring along edge of glove and work 80 sc over elastic and into loops. Join with ss.

Rnd 28: Ch 3, 1 dc in each st to end, join with ss.

Rnd 29: Ch 3, 3 dc, *ch 4, skip 3 sts, 1 sc, ch 4, skip 3 sts, 4 dc, rep from * to end, omitting last 4 dc, join with ss.

Rnd 30: Ch 3, 3 dc, *ch 4, 1 sc in sc, ch 4, 4 dc, rep from * to end, omitting last 4 dc, join with ss.

Rnd 31: Ch 3, 3 dc, *(ch 4, 1 sc in next ch sp) twice, ch 4, 4 dc, rep from * to end, omitting last 4 dc, join with ss.

Rnd 32: Ch 3, 3 dc, *(ch 4, 1 sc in sc) twice, ch 4, 4 dc, rep from * to end, omitting last 4 dc, join with ss.

Rnd 33: Ch 3, 3 dc, *ch 7, skip ch-1 sp, 1 sc, in next ch sp, skip ch-1 sp, ch 7, 4 dc, rep from * to end, omitting last 4 dc, join with ss.

Rnd 34: *(4 sc, 1 picot, 4 sc) in ch-7 sp, rep from * to end. Join with ss. Fasten off.

Right Hand

Work as for left hand until 4 fingers are joined, and third round of hand is completed.

Rnd 4: Mark commencement of rnds at side of glove to correspond with left hand glove. That is, mark opposite side of hand for thumb insertion. Complete this glove as for left hand, incorporating thumb as

The finished gloves.

before, but on opposite side of palm of hand.

Make 2 small flowers such as the small Irish rose on page 85. Sew one of these firmly to each glove, just above the elastic at center back of hand.

Press the finished pair of gloves into shape under a damp cloth.

Tenerife Lace Bedspread

If made using No. 10 or No. 8 crochet cotton
and a large hook size, such as a 1.75 or 2.00
mm (size 6 or 4/5), this pattern is ideal for a
bedspread. Make as many of the motifs as
required for the size of bed. These are linked
together after the circles are made, not during
the final round as usual.

Another way to copy Tenerife lace is by using a
daisy loom. Once again, make as many motifs
as required on the daisy loom for the bed being
covered, working with yarn rather than thread.

Materials:

For a single bedspread, you will need
approximately 32 x 50 g balls (approx.
7200 yds.) of No. 10 crochet cotton.

Place the circles so that they lie in rows.

Stage 1: Join the circles together as
follows: Join yarn to a loop from the daisy
or the ch 3 loop in the Tenerife motif, *ch 3,
1 sc in next loop. When the loop is reached
that touches another motif, work the 1 sc
through both circles at once. That is, put
the wrong sides of the circles together and
treat the loops from both motifs as one.

Stage 2: To save having to break off the
thread too much, it is possible to work
around half of each circle until a whole
strip of circles has been joined together on
one side only.

Stage 3: As you continue around the circles
to complete the strip, the bottom half of the
second strip will also be joined. Continue
working the ch 3, 1 sc in each loop on each
circle, joining them together where they
meet. This method also frames the whole
bedspread at the time of joining, and with a
minimum number of ends to secure.

Bedspread made using the daisy loom method.

Chapter Seven
Edgings

Edgings

Edgings, along with motifs, were probably some of the first pieces of crochet produced. Lace edgings were very popular for underwear, caps, frivolities, fabric ruffles, handkerchiefs, household linen, and so on, and crochet was a quick way to produce something similar to real lace. Because crochet was copying lace, those who had the money to buy the real thing used to ridicule the new craft and until the middle of the twentieth century, crochet had to suffer two derogatory nicknames: "poor man's lace" and "nun's lace."

During the nineteenth century, Lancashire was producing much of the cotton thread in Britain. When it was discovered that crochet could use a larger amount of cotton more quickly than lace, the distributors placed a simple edging pattern inside the ball band wrapper to encourage more people to purchase their products. However, as has been pointed out before, not everyone could follow a pattern and therefore the manufacturers found another way to attract customers

In the early twentieth century, a manufacturer would pay a home-worker to crochet samples of their edging designs. These samples were then sold along with the cotton purchased to make the article. The purchaser would first continue direct from the sample to ensure the tension was correct before proceeding with the whole length. Frequently there would be no crochet hook size suggested. This was not a problem, however, as crochet is extremely easy to undo and the thread can be reused over and over again. So it did not matter how many times a trial continuation of the sample piece was practiced. The worst that could happen was that the work would become soiled. (Remember that the hook was shaped and the tension could be made larger by moving the finger further along the hook away from the hook head. Conversely, to tighten the tension, the finger acting as a stop needed to go closer to the hook head.)

The most popular sample pieces purchased were those including a crocheted corner since this meant that square and rectangular cloths could have attractive edgings of crocheted lace added. You can often pick up these tiny sample pieces with a ticket attached giving the price of 1d (one old English penny) for a medium-width straight edging, going up to the princely sum of 3d for a wider edging with corner.

Edgings for Today

The most popular use of thread crochet today is for edgings and trimmings, along with doilies and table centers. The patterns have not really changed. When it comes to edgings in thread crochet, the old saying, "There is nothing new, but just a remembering of something that was," is very apt. However, the designs are innumerable and this left me in a difficult position when trying to choose just a few to include here. I hope you enjoy the ones I eventually selected.

Attaching an Edging

Once an edging is completed there has to be a way of attaching it to the fabric of the item for which it was made. The most common complaint about crocheted edgings on handkerchiefs, tablecloths, tray cloths and so on is that they seem to break away from the fabric after frequent laundering. To prevent this from happening, I suggest you attach the edging with a finer gauge of the same kind of mercerized thread that was used to make the edging. (Normally people use sewing cotton to attach the edging, which is weaker than the crochet thread.) Mercerized crochet thread has a tight twist and an additional finish that makes it exceptionally hard wearing and resistant to the negative effects of sunlight. This is one reason why there was a generation gap in producing household linen and edgings—articles produced by mothers and grandmothers seem to go on forever.

Sewing Method

Choosing the thread: The weight of the crochet should be similar to that of the fabric to which it will be attached, so if you are adding a crochet edging to lingerie, you may need to use silk thread rather than mercerized cotton. In this instance, the crochet requires sewing to the fabric with the thread that you used to make the edging.

Fitting the edging: If a repeat pattern is large, there is a tendency to want to stretch the fabric to make it fit the crochet edging. It is always prudent to make an additional pattern before running a cotton thread through the row of crochet or the edge of the crochet strip. Use this thread to ease the crochet evenly onto the fabric. The edging will lie and hang better if the edging is a tiny bit longer than the fabric when the pattern dictates that the fit is not perfect.

Attaching the edging: Use small, even stitches to sew the crochet edge to the article.

Crochet Method

Drawn-thread hem: Sometimes it is difficult to buy handkerchiefs with a drawn-thread hem close to the edge. These are not readily available, but you may find a supplier among the list of useful addresses at the end of this book. If you do have a drawn-thread hem on the fabric, it is a very simple matter to insert your hook into the hole and work a row of either 1 single crochet and chain 1 per hole or 2 single crochet in each hole. Depending on your tension, you may find that you can work 2 single crochet in one hole but only 1 sc in the next. There is no hard-and-fast rule for the number of stitches required. Instead please use your own common sense. Do not try to make the sc or sc and ch fit the holes – the top edge of your stitches should fall exactly on the edge of the fabric.

Closely woven fabric: When working with a closely woven fabric, such as cotton or linen, you can use a sewing machine to make faux drawn-thread work. Fit the largest available machine needle (the kind used for upholstery fabric) into the machine, leaving the needle unthreaded. Set the longest stitch size and run the fabric edge under the sewing machine needle, allowing it to punch holes. This creates a drawn-thread effect into which you can then insert a fine crochet hook.

Other fabrics: For other fabrics or thicker yarns and thread, embroider a chain evenly along the edge of the fabric and use each chain as though it were the top of a stitch. However, if you are working a long length, you may find your chain stitches get progressively bigger. Please avoid this; otherwise you will find all kinds of problems emerge when you try to get the edges to match or the length of crochet to hang evenly from the fabric.

Working Corners

Designing your own: Many patterns for edgings or insertion strips do not have a corner pattern but this does not mean you can't make a corner for yourself. To make a corner from a straight edging, place an unframed mirror on the work diagonally at right angles as shown below. Let the mirror travel along the whole length of the pattern before deciding which part of the design will produce the most pleasing corner. Then either work from the mirror to make the corner or, if the edging is in filet, rechart it.

Working the next side: In most instances it is possible to reverse the design for the corner and then continue following the original pattern. However, if the edging includes sprays of flowers that are not symmetrical, the whole of the second side to the next corner will have to be worked in reverse. In filet edgings, I find recharting to be the best method as it tends to avoid any hidden snags.

Insertion strips: It is unusual to require a corner in an insertion strip, but if one is needed the same procedure applies.

Number of stitches: The only additional piece of information you need to crochet the edge directly from the fabric is the number of stitches it will require. For a two-stitch pattern, you will need an odd number of stitches in the base row of single crochet or single crochet and chain that has been worked from the drawn-thread hem edge, the sewn chain edge, or the holes punched along the fabric edge by the sewing machine.

Using a mirror to create a corner design.

Edging Patterns

Here are some edging patterns for you to try. The first six edgings—the mock-picot edge, puff-stitch edge, the two open-shell edgings, castle edging, and tent-panel edging—are narrow and are designed to be worked directly from the fabric; the arched edge, trefoil, open-diamond, and victory edge are wider but can also be worked directly from the fabric, while the simple fan-stitch border, Estelle crocheted edging, braided panel edge, arches, and Irish edging should be made independently and then attached to the fabric when completed.

Mock-Picot Edge

One row only: Start with an odd number of sts. With WS facing, ch 1, *1 tr, 1 sc, rep from * to end. Fasten off.

Puff-Stitch Edge

One row only: Start with an odd number of sts. With RS facing, ch 3, *(yo, insert hook into next st, yo, draw the loop through, lifting the loop until it is level with the top of the ch 3) 4 times, yo, pull through all 9 loops [1 puff stitch made], ch 1, skip 1 st, rep from * to last st, 1 tr in last st. Fasten off.

Optional edge: With RS facing, work 1 row of crab stitches.

Open-Shell Edge

One row only: Start with a number of stitches that is divisible by 8 with 1 left over. With RS facing, ch 1, *skip 3 sts, ch 1, (1 tr, ch 1) 5 times in next st, skip 3 sts, 1 ss in next st, rep from * to end. Fasten off.

Open-Shell Edge with Picot

One row only: Start with a number of stitches that is divisible by 6 with 1 left over. Ch 1, *skip 2 sts, (3 dc, 1 picot, 3 dc) in next st, skip 2 sts, 1 ss in next st, rep from * to end. Fasten off.

Castle Edge for Ribbon

One row only: Start with a number of stitches that is divisible by 4 with 2 left over. With RS facing, ch 2, 1 hdc in next st, *ch 6, 1 dc in fourth ch from hook, (1 dc in next ch) twice, skip 2 sts, 2 hdc, rep from * to end. Fasten off. Ribbon can be slotted through this edging.

Tent-Pattern Edge

Row 1: Start with a number of stitches that is divisible by 8 with 1 left over. Ch 4, 2 dc in fifth ch from hook (or first st), *skip 3 sts, 1 sc, skip 3 sts, (2 dc, ch 3, 2 dc) in next st, rep from * to last 8 sts, skip 3 sts, 1 sc, skip 3 sts, (2 dc, ch 1, 1 dc) in last st.

Row 2: *Ch 4, 1 p, 4 dc cl (worked in 4 separate dc), ch 4, 1 p, 1 sc in ch-3 sp, rep from * to end. Fasten off.

Arched Edge

Row 1: Start with a number of stitches that is divisible by 3 with 1 left over. Ch 3, *skip 2 sts, ch 2, 1 dc in next st, rep from * to end.

Row 2: *Ch 3, 1 dc in ch-2 sp, ch 3, 7 dc in sp between ch 3 and dc of this row, 1 sc in dc of row 1, rep from * to end. Fasten off.

Open Diamond

Row 1: Start with a number of stitches that is divisible by 6 with 1 left over. Ch 1, sc to end.

Row 2: Ch 6, *skip 3 sts, (1 tr, ch 1) 3 times in next st, skip 5 sts, rep from * to last 2 sts, (1 tr, ch 1) twice in next st, 1 unfinished tr [2 loops on hook] in same place, 1 unfinished dtr [3 loops on hook] in last st, yo, draw through all 3 loops.

Row 3: Ch 6, *[next 5 sts are all unfinished to form a cluster] 1 dtr in same place, 3 dc cl in central tr, 1 dtr in sp bet groups, yo, draw through all 6 loops, ch 5, rep from * to end, reducing last ch 5 to ch 3, 1 tr in last st.

Row 4: Ch 1, 1 sc in same place, ch 16, (1 p, 1 sc) in ch-3 sp, *ch 5, 1 sc in ch-5 sp, two 6-ch p in same place, 1 sc in same place, rep from * to end, omitting second p. Fasten off.

Trefoil Edge

Row 1: Start with a number of stitches that is divisible by 8 with 5 left over. Ch 1, 1 sc in same place, *skip 3 sts (1 puff st, ch 2) twice, 1 puff st all in the next st, skip 3 sts, 1 sc, rep from * to last 4 sts, skip 3 sts, (1 puff st, ch 2, 1 thin puff st) in last st.

Row 2: Ch 1, 1 sc in same place, ch 2, *3 dc in sc, ch 2, 1 sc in center puff st, ch 2, rep from * to last st, 2 dc in last st.

Row 3: Ch 3, 1 pulled up dc in same place, ch 2, 1 puff st still in same place, *1 sc in sc, (1 puff st, ch 2) twice, 1 puff st in center of gr, rep from * to last st, 1 sc in last st. Fasten off.

Victory Edge

Row 1: Start with a number of sts that is divisible by 5 with 1 left over. Ch 3, 1 dc in each st to end.

Row 2: Ch 4, skip 1 st, *(1 dc, ch 3, 1 dc) in next st, ch 3, skip 4 sts, rep from * to last 4 sts, (1 dc, ch 3, 1 dc) in next st, ch 1, 1 dc in last st.

Row 3: Ch 7, (2 tr cl, ch 5, 2 tr cl) in center sp of gr, ch 4, rep from * to end, 1 dtr in last st.

Row 4: Ch 1, 1 sc in same place *ch 1, (1 hdc, 1 dc, 1 tr, 1 dtr, 1 tr, 1 dc, 1 hdc) in ch-5 sp, ch 1, 1 sc in ch-4 sp, rep from * to end. Fasten off.

Simple Fan-Stitch Border

Ch 40 [depth of edge].

Row 1: (1 dc, ch 2, 2 dc) in fourth ch from hook, *ch 5, skip ch 8, (2 dc, ch 2, 2 dc) in next ch, rep from * to end, ch 3, turn.

Row 2: *(2 dc, ch 2, 2 dc) in ch-2 sp, ch 4, 2 dc on dc, (2 dc, ch 2, 2 dc) in ch-2 sp, 2 dc, rep from * once, (2 dc, ch 2, 2 dc) in ch-2 sp, ch 3, turn.

Row 3: *(2 dc, ch 2, 2 dc) in ch-2 sp, ch 3, 4 dc, (2 dc, ch 2, 2 dc) in ch-2 sp, 4 dc, ch 3, rep from * once, (2 dc, ch 2, 2 dc) in ch-2 sp, ch 3, turn.

Row 4: *(2 dc, ch 2, 2 dc) in ch-2 sp, ch 5, rep from * to end, omitting last ch 5, ch 3, turn.

Subsequent rows: Rep rows 2–4 for length required, finishing with following row to replace last row 4 worked: Ss to ch-2 sp, 1 sc in ch-2 sp, *ch 8, 1 sc in ch-2 sp, rep from * to end.

Note: To make a firmer edge for towels, work 1 row sc over chains in the first and final rows.

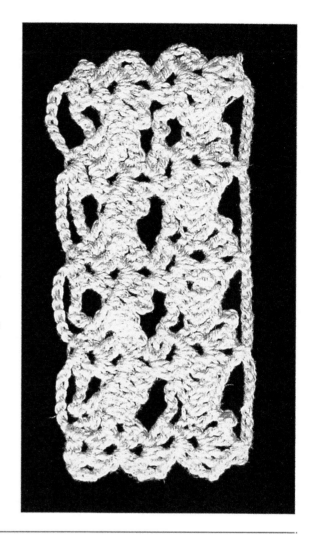

Estelle Crocheted Edging

Ch 11, join into a ring with ss. Ch 3, 11 dc in ring. Turn work so that wrong side of dc is facing.

Row 1: Ch 10, skip 4 sts, 1 dc, ch 3, skip 2 sts, 1 dc, ch 3, skip 2 st, 1 dc, turn.

Row 2: Ch 5, skip 2 ch, 3 dc, ch 3, skip 3 st, 1 dc in each of the 3 ch, ch 3, skip 2 st, 11 dc in the ch 10 made on row 1.

Subsequent rows: Repeat rows 1 and 2 until sufficient length has been achieved.

Braided Panel Edge

To make this edging, you first need to work a length of braid to substitute for the machine-made braids of the nineteenth century. Then you add a lace filling to make an arched panel. Second and subsequent lengths of braid should be made into arched panels and attached as they are being worked.

To make the braid, ch 10, 1 dc in sixth ch from hook, 4 dc, *ch 5, turn, 5 dc, rep from * 42 times, ch 2.

To make the filling, ch 10, (skip ch-5 loop, 1 sc in next loop) 4 times, (ch 1, 1 sc in next loop) 6 times, (ch 10, skip 1 loop, 1 sc in next loop) 4 times, ch 2, (13 sc in ch-10 loop) 4 times, 1 sc in each ch-1 loop, (7 sc, ss to center sc of 13 sc opposite 6 sc) 4 times, ch 2, 5 dc to complete length of braid. Fasten off.

Row 2: Ch 10, 1 dc in sixth ch from hook, 4 dc, *ch 2, ss to first outer loop on last braid, ch 2, 5 dc, ch 5, turn, 5 dc, rep from * 8 times. Rep row 2 another 25 times [i.e. to length of first braid], rep from * to end.

Subsequent rows: Continue adding arches to length required.

Final row: [Along the straight side] ch 6, 1 dc in first of 5 dc, ch 3, 1 dc in ch-2 sp, ch 3, 1 tr in second sc of loop, 1 tr in next to last sc of next large loop, ch 3, 1 dc in ch sp, ch 3, 1 dc in first of 5 dc, ch 3, 1 dc in last of 5 dc, rep to end. Fasten off.

Arches

Ch 13.

Row 1: 1 dc in fourth ch from hook, 2 dc, ch 3, skip 3 ch, 4 dc, ch 3, turn.

Row 2: *3 dc, ch 3, skip 3 ch, 4 dc**, ch 3, turn.

Rows 3–8: Rep row 2.

Row 9: Work as row 2 from * to **, ch 8, ss to base of turning ch on row 8, ch 3, turn.

Row 10: 8 dc, ch 3, 10 dc in ch-8 sp, work from * to ** of row 2, ch 3, turn.

Row 11: Work as row 2 from * to **, ch 7, (3 dc, ch 3, 3 dc) in ch-3 sp, ch 7, ss to base of ch on row 6, ch 3, turn.

Row 12: 12 dc in ch-7 sp, ch 2 (3 dc, ch 3, 3 dc) in ch-3 sp, ch 2, 14 dc, work as row 2 from * to **, ch 3, turn.

Row 13: Work as row 2 from * to **, ch 8, 3 dc in ch-2 sp, ch 3, (3 dc, ch 3, 3 dc) in ch-3 sp, ch 3, 3 dc in ch-2 sp, ch 8, ss to base of ch 3 on row 4.

Row 14: 16 dc in ch-8 sp, 6 dc in ch-3 sp, (3 dc, ch 1, 1 p, ch 1, 3 dc) in next ch-3 sp, 6 dc in next sp, 18 dc in ch-8 sp, as row 2 from * to **.

Rows 15–16: Rep row 2.

Subsequent rows: Rep rows 3–16 for length required.

Note: For a firmer edge, work an extra row of dc.

Irish Edging for Linen

Row 1: Ch 7, and catch with a sc into edge of cloth. Rep all around, allowing very little fullness for each loop as these stand off in curves when sc is added in next row.

Row 2: Work over each loop of ch 7 below, *3 sc, ch 4 for picot, 8 sc [close crocheters can get in 9 sc], catch into edge of cloth. Rep from *.

Row 3: *Ch 7, catch into center of loop below. Rep from *.

Row 4: Rep row 2.

Row 5: Rep row 3.

Row 6: Into first loop, work *3 sc, ch 4 for p, 6 sc, ch 4 for p, 3 sc, catch into point below. Into next loop, work 3 sc, ch 4 for p, 3 sc, ch 7, turn back and catch it into center of sc in previous loop. Into this ch 7, work 3 sc, ch 4 for p, 2 sc, ch 4 for p, 2 sc, ch 4 for p, 3 sc. This brings you back to the half-worked loop below at the point where you turned back. Now go straight on and complete the half-worked loop with 3 sc, ch 4 for p, 3 sc, catch into point below. Rep from *. Fasten off.

Projects

Make a curtain edging and matching tiebacks, or a pretty summer top, using the techniques described here.

Summer Top Edging

What could be quicker than transforming an off-the-rack top into something exclusive by adding this little edging? Alternatively, you could use a glitter yarn for an evening event.

Ch 8.

Row 1: 1 ss in fifth ch from hook (1 p made), *ch 10, 1 ss in fifth ch from hook (1 p made), rep from * to desired length, ch 4. Fasten off.

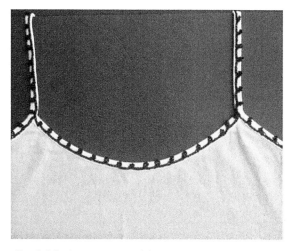

The finished summer top edging.

Voile Curtain Edging and Tieback

Edgings can be placed on all sorts of things, from clothing to curtains. This edging has been adapted to make a tieback which is in keeping with the rest of the curtain. It is worked sideways.

Curtain Edging

Ch 8.

Row 1: 1 dc in fourth ch from hook, 2 dc, ch 2, skip 1 st, (1 dc, ch 2) 3 times all in next st, 1 sc in same st, ch 1, turn.

Row 2: (1 sc, 2 dc, 1 sc) in next ch-2 sp, (1 sc, 3 dc, ch 2, 3 dc, 1 sc) in next ch sp, (1 sc, 2 dc, 1 sc) in next ch sp, skip next ch sp, 4 dc, ch 3, turn.

Row 3: 3 dc, ch 2, skip ch-1 sp, (1 dc, ch 2) 3 times in ch-2 sp, 1 dc in same loop, ch 1, turn.

Row 4: (1 sc, 2 dc, 1 sc) in next ch sp, (1 sc, 3 dc, ch 2, 3 dc, 1 sc) in next ch sp, (1 sc, 2 dc, 1 sc) in next ch sp, ch 2, skip next ch-2 sp, 4 dc, ch 3, turn.

Rep rows 3 and 4 to desired length. On last row, omit ch 3.

Working back across edging, ch 1, *1 sc in each of the ch created as a turning ch, ch 3, skip dc row end, rep from * to end, 1 sc in last st. Fasten off.

Tieback

Work as for edging to desired length.

At each end of the tieback, place 3 sc, ch 4, 3 sc to form a loop. Fasten off.

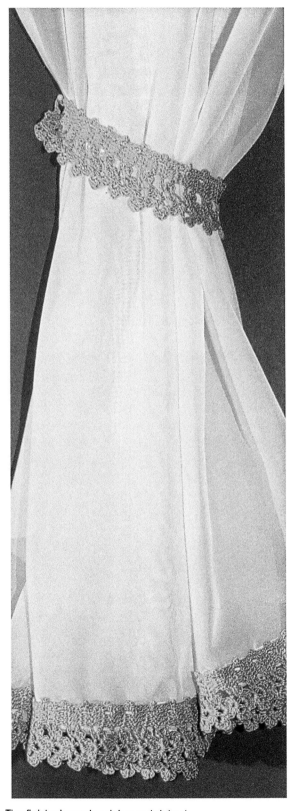

The finished curtain edging and tieback.

Chapter Eight
Adaptation and Finishing

Adaptation and Finishing

Earlier in this book, you probably noticed numerous tips on how to use stitches and designs to make a variety of articles. The one area that has not been extensively covered in this respect is the world of fashion.

Crochet is still the one textile that cannot be reproduced by machine, and with its recurrent presence on the catwalks of Paris, London, and New York among others, it is inevitable that more people are being employed in the Third World to produce the crochet garments that fashion demands.

However, when crochet was a new craft, very little was produced for the fashion industry, and those items that were available were usually limited to trimmings and underwear, which particularly lent itself to fine-thread crochet. Wool and yarn crochet emerged later and were often worked on hooks that were too small for the yarn, making them stiff, heavy, and often ungainly. Children's coats, for instance, were so stiff that it was almost impossible to bend the arms, making them more like straightjackets than coats! Fortunately, as the twentieth century receded and the twenty-first century began, crochet became a prominent feature in fashion.

When high-fashion shops started stocking lacy designs that appealed to young and old alike, it brought back thread as a medium for fashion articles instead of the yarn that had dominated fashion crochet over the previous three decades. The joy of fashion crochet is its ability to be timeless, while at the same time having patterns that can be easily adapted to whatever trend is in fashion. I have selected a few items to act as a source of inspiration.

This delightful patterned chiffon top hangs well because of the cotton edging that was worked directly into the fabric.

A simple lacy pattern originally used for a cotton curtain looks stunning as a sleeveless top, using a fashion yarn that has been spun with a hint of a glint.

Here a fine Lurex thread was chosen to match the machine embroidery that edges the embroidered leaves. The fabric is so fragile that it was necessary to embroider a chain around the whole piece before the edging was added. At the underarm seam position the edging was linked during the last row of the crochet, precisely as one would join motifs. This avoids additional ends in a yarn that is very slippery and which needs to be carefully secured if it is to prevent any possibility of the edge unravelling.

A fine machine-knit yarn was worked into knitted panels to create a design feature and interesting godets for shape in this eight-gored skirt. Where the fashion trend is for slits rather than flares, the same idea can be used but without the godets, simply joining two, four or eight panels down to the base, leaving one, two or four slit openings for movement.

Thinking Laterally

During my travels as a teacher and lecturer I am often asked for crocheted collar patterns. As crochet for fashion became popular the demand for all kinds of wearing apparel, including accessories, outstripped the printing of crochet designs. However, the often-used expression "Why reinvent the wheel?" comes to mind—there are numerous doilies worked around damask and linen circles that can be adapted into delightful collar designs for numerous different kinds of garments.

When and How to Press (or Not)

Pressing crochet is not normally recommended because it flattens the texture of the stitches. Certainly mixed fibers and some silks are best left to themselves and an iron or other pressing equipment should be kept well away unless it is absolutely necessary. There are always exceptions to any rules, however, and as this book is dealing primarily with thread that includes both cotton and linen, I need to reverse my normal statement of "Please do not press" and suggest that when using 100%-cotton or linen thread, you do press.

Cotton crochet normally looks better if it has been pressed, particularly when the edge has picots, points, or some other decorative edge that requires a little extra attention to prevent curling after laundering. The other occasion on which you may find it necessary to press crochet is when joining shapes together. No matter how careful you are with your tension, there is a possibility of the shapes being ever so slightly different in size to each other. This is often the case if you find you have to change the actual hook you have been working with, even if it is the same size, or if you have had to leave the work for some length of time. I find block pressing ideal for ensuring everything in the piece of work is the same size.

To block press, pin the work onto a blanket, starting from the center of each side or from four quarters of a circle. Make sure that the pinheads nestle into the blanket and not into the crochet. You can even outline the size of the motif using a colorfast sewing thread or with pins. This will be necessary for motifs that have to be all the same size. Continue to pin on each side, working in opposite pairs.

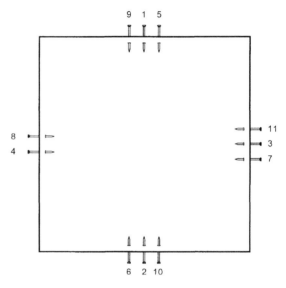

Insert pins for the preparation of block pressing in the order shown here.

Cover the pinned-out article with a damp cloth. Be careful to use something like an old white cotton pillowcase, large handkerchief, white tea towel, or tablecloth for this process or you could create irreparable damage with dye stains. Mercerized cotton does not absorb dye as easily as cotton that is not mercerized, but nevertheless the danger is there. Use a hot iron and press over the cloth. Do not move the iron as you would when ironing; just press firmly, lift, and then move to another part of the damp fabric and press again until the fabric covering the motif or article is dry. Remove the cloth. Without steam and from a distance of about 2 to 5 cm (¾" to 2") above the work, let the iron move lightly over the crochet to aid drying. Leave the crochet pinned out until completely dry, when it can be removed from the blanket.

Large items can be treated this way on a double thickness of blanket placed on the floor. Find a time or space without children or animal interference. Once the damp cloth has been removed, cover with a dry cloth and place in a safe place (under a bed, for example) until the drying is completed.

Lining

On the whole, crochet does not require lining, but occasionally thread crochet can be enhanced with a contrast background. If you feel that lining will improve your work, the following guidelines can help. For simplicity, I have divided them into two sections. Working with thread crochet for fashion items requires a different approach to that used when using thread crochet for household items.

Lining Fashion Items

Minimal stitching: Attach the lining at as few points as possible.

Movement allowance: Make the lining larger than the pieces of crochet since there is less give in lining material than in crochet fabric and a movement allowance needs to be included.

Color check: Be extremely careful when purchasing the lining that the color is complementary to the crochet, both in daylight and artificial light. Even in double crochet there are minute holes through which the lining may show, particularly with a garment that may be worn on a dance floor.

Dealing with sleeves: Attach sleeve linings only at the armhole edge unless there is a deep, tight cuff on each sleeve.

Full lining: Attach a full lining for the trunk of the body only at neck and armholes.

Skirt lining: Attach a skirt lining only at the waistband. If it is attached to the hem the crochet tends to react in an unpredictable way, usually twisting in the opposite direction to the lining material.

Lining Household Items

Pillows: Pillow inserts should be larger than the crocheted cover for a plump appearance and to act as a lining.

Picture motifs: Picture motifs look good on velvet or coarse, even-weave material. Tiny, very even stitches need to be used to attach the crochet to the background so that they can't be seen when the picture is on the wall.

Bed throws: These are best kept loose and thrown over a single-color coverlet. Satin is lovely, but unless the bedspread is very heavy it could slide off. Velvet is often too heavy as a lining so a contemporary, vibrant-colored sheet may be the answer.

Braids

The braids given here are simple to make and will provide attractive edgings for any garment.

Narrow Braid

Strange things happen to this braid if a contrasting thick chain or cord is threaded through the center holes. You may wish to use it as an alternative to some of the machine-made braids of yesteryear. The braid can also be used as a ribbon.

Ch 2, 1 sc in first ch, *ch 2, turn, 1 sc in same place as turning ch. Rep from * for required length.

Puff-Stitch Braid

This braid is effective as an additional edging.

Make a chain of an odd number. *(Yo, insert hook into ch, yo, pull through loop to front) 4 times, yo, pull through all loops on hook (1 puff st made), 1 ss in next ch, rep from * to length required.

Rickrack Braid

This braid can be incorporated into an article since it is worked by attaching one side using ch 2, 1 ss into work, ch 2.

Ch 5, 1 sc in fifth ch from hook, turn, *ch 4, 1 sc in sc of previous row, turn. Rep from * for required length.

Vetch Braid

This braid is ideal for giving a scalloped edge to a design with irregular sides.

Ch 8, join with 1 ss to form a ring, ch 3, 7 dc in ring, ch 6, sc in ring, turn, *ch 3, 7 dc in ch-6 sp, ch 6, sc in ch-6 sp, turn, rep from * to length required.

From left to right: narrow braid, puff-stitch braid, rickrack braid, vetch braid and narrow braid with contrasting chain.

Projects

Here are a selection of simple buttons to make and a more ambitious project—a Victorian collar. Making your own buttons for a crocheted garment is an excellent idea. Not only will they look good but also they will probably be lighter than those you can buy. Certainly they will make laundering simpler, because they will be of the same thread as the article you have crocheted.

All buttons have a tighter center when worked as described, with the tail end drawing up the first chain. Make sure the cover is taut.

Bullion Stitch Button

Rnd 1: Ch 4, *wind yarn 10 times around hook, insert hook into first of ch 4 made, bring yarn through the chain, yo, draw this yarn through all 12 loops in one movement [a tambour-shaped hook helps in this process], ch 1 to close bullion st, rep from * 9 times, ss to top of ch 4.

Rnd 2: Ch 1, *1 sc in top of bullion st, 1 sc in back loop of ch, rep from * to end, join with ss, turn.

Rnd 3: Ch 1, *2 sc, sc2tog, rep from * to end [15 sts], turn.

Rnd 4: Ch 1, *1 sc, sc2tog, rep from * to end. Insert the mold before completing this round. Finish off with a long thread to

Clockwise from top: crochet-covered bead, crochet-covered flat button, bullion stitch button.

gather through last row of sts. Draw up firmly and stitch securely to attach button to garment.

Crochet-Covered Bead

This is an ideal button for bridal and confirmation gowns.

Ch 3, 9 dc in first of these chains, ss to join. Leave 20 cm (8") to gather around inserted bead and attach to article.

Crochet-Covered Flat Button

Ch 2, 8 sc in first ch, do not join, 2 hdc in each sc to end.

If the button or mold you are covering is larger than the crochet now made, work an additional round of either sc or hdc. Thread a 20 cm (8") yarn through each st.

Stretch the cover over the mold or button and draw firmly up before finishing off. Use the shank of the inside mold or button to attach the finished button to the crocheted garment.

Victorian Collar

This high-necked collar is typical of the Victorian period, when lace collars, insertions, yokes, and jabots were frequently found on women's clothing.

Materials:

• 2 x 50 g balls (approx. 570 yds.) of No. 20 cotton DMC

• 1.25 mm (size 9 or 10) crochet hook for small neck; 150 mm (size 7 or 8) crochet hook for medium neck; 1.75 mm (size 6) crochet hook for large neck

• Narrow ribbon

Ch 123.

Row 1: 1 dc in fourth ch from hook, 1 dc in each ch to end [121 sts].

Row 2: Ch 5, trtr, *ch 5, skip 5 sts, 2 trtr, rep from * to end, ch 3, turn.

Row 3: Dc to end, ch 4, turn.

Row 4: Skip 2 sts, 1 sc in next st, *ch 3, skip 2 sts, 1 sc, rep from * to end, ch 4, turn.

Row 5: 1 sc in sp, *ch 3, (1 sc, ch 3, 1 sc) in next sp, ch 3, 1 sc in next st, rep from * to last sp, ch 3 (1 sc, ch 3, 1 sc) in last sp.

Row 6: Work as row 5.

The neck stand is complete but do not break off the yarn at this stage. Continue down the edge with (ch 3, 1 sc) to make edge similar to that of last row of neck stand.

Main Collar

Work into the foundation chain again:

Row 1: Ch 5, 1 sc in sixth st, *ch 5, skip 4 sts, 1 sc in next st, rep from * to end.

Row 2: *Ch 5, 1 sc in sp, ch 2, 3 dc cl in sc, ch 2, 1 sc in sp, rep from * to last sp, ch 5, 1 sc in center of ch of last sp [into actual stitch].

Row 3: Ch 5, 1 sc in sp, *ch 1, 3 tr cl in cl, ch 4, 1 ss in cl, ch 4, 3 tr cl in cl, ch 1, 1 sc in sp, ch 5, 1 sc in same sp, rep from * to end [with last sc being worked in center st of sp].

Row 4: *Ch 5, 1 sc in sp, ch 5, 1 sc in cl, ch 2, 3 tr cl in ss, ch 2, 1 sc in cl, rep from * to last sp, ch 5, 1 sc in sp, ch 3, 1 dc in same sp.

Row 5: Ch 5, 1 sc in sp, *ch 5, 1 sc in cl, ch 5, 1 sc in sp, ch 5, 1 sc in same sp, rep from * to end, ch 3, 1 dc in last sp.

Row 6: *Ch 5, 1 sc in sp, rep from * to end, ch 2, 1 dc in last sp.

Row 7: *Ch 2, 3 dc cl in sc, ch 2, 1 sc in sp, ch 5, 1 sc in next sp, ch 5, 1 sc in same sp, ch 5, 1 sc in next sp, rep from * to last sp, ch 2, 3 dc cl in sc, ch 2, 1 sc in last sp, ch 2, 1 dc in end, ch 1, turn.

Row 8: *Ch 1, 3 tr cl in cl, ch 4, 1 ss in cl, ch 4, 3 tr cl in cl, ch 1, 1 sc in sp, (ch 5, 1 sc in next sp) twice, rep from * to last cl, ch 1, 3 tr cl in cl, ch 4, 1 ss in cl, ch 4, 3 tr cl in cl, ch 1, 1 sc to end.

Row 9: *Ch 2, 3 dc cl in ss, ch 2, 1 sc in next cl, (ch 5, 1 sc) twice, 1 sc in cl, rep from * to last ss, ch 2, 3 dc cl in ss, ch 2, 1 sc in cl.

Row 10: Ch 7, 1 sc in cl, *(ch 5, 1 sc in sp) twice, ch 5, 1 sc in same sp, ch 5, 1 sc in same sp, ch 5, 1 sc in cl, rep from * to end, ch 4, 1 tr in end.

Row 11: *Ch 5, 1 sc in next sp, rep from * to last sp, ch 3, 1 tr.

Row 12: (Ch 5, 1 sc in next sp) 4 times, rep from * to last 3 sps, ch 1, 3 dc cl in next sc, ch 1, ch 1, 1 sc in sp, (ch 5, 1 sc in next sp) twice, ch 3, 1 tr in end.

Row 13: (Ch 5, 1 sc in next sp) twice *ch 1, 3 tr cl in cl, ch 4, 1 ss in same place, ch 4, 3 tr cl, ch 1, 1 sc in next sp (ch 5, 1 sc in next sp) 3 times, rep from * to last cl, ch 1, 3 tr cl in cl, ch 4, 1 ss in the same place, ch 3, 3 tr cl, ch 1, 1 sc in next sp, (ch 5, 1 sc) twice, ch 3, 1 tr in end.

Row 14: (Ch 5, 1 sc in next sp) twice, ch 5, 1 sc in cl, *ch 2, 3 tr cl in ss, ch 2, 1 sc in ch, (ch 5, 1 sc in next sp) 4 times, rep from * to last 2 sps, (ch 5, 1 sc in sp) twice, ch 3, 1 tr in last st.

Row 15: Ch 5, 1 sc in sp (ch 5, 1 sc in next sp, ch 5, 1 sc in same sp) twice, *(ch 5, 1 sc in ch-2 sp) twice, (ch 5, 1 sc in next sp, ch 5, 1 sc in same sp) 6 times, rep from * to last 3 sps, (ch 5, 1 sc in next sp, ch 5, 1 sc in same sp) twice, ch 5, 1 sc in last sp.

Row 16: *Ch 5, 1 sc in next sp, ch 5, 1 sc in same sp, ch 5, 1 sc in next sp, rep from * to end, ch 5, 1 sc in last st.v

Side Edge

Without breaking the yarn, work up this side of the collar in sc, keeping a straight edge, ch 1, turn and work 1 sc in each stitch down to the end of the collar.

Row 17: *Ch 4, 1 sc in next sp, ch 4, 1 sc in same place, ch 4, 1 sc in next sp, rep from * to end.

Final Side Edge

Either work in sc as the other side or continue in tiny loops as at the neck. Fasten off.

Thread the ribbon through the collar. Use snaps for a neat fastener or have extra ribbon to be used as a tie.

The finished Victorian collar.

Index

About the Author

Pauline Turner is the author of many books
and articles on crochet, including *How to
Crochet*, published by Collins & Brown, and
runs an international correspondence course,
the Diploma in Crochet, the first part of which
has also been adapted for the City and Guilds
in the UK. She is a founding member of the
Knitting and Crochet Guild of Great Britain
and is the International Liaison Chairperson of
the Crochet Guild of America.